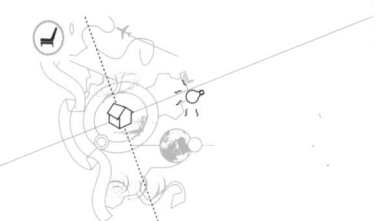

Intro

As part of the new School of Architecture & Design, we now have a looser relationship with Furniture, and more evenly spread contacts with Industrial Design and Computer Related Design.

This reflects the fact that architecture as a practice is increasingly intertwined with other design activities - the approach to the Millennium, its apocalyptic and feverish undertow aside, is moving towards the integration of programme and spatial container, event and building. Architecture is an art of communication alongside graphics and advertising, but it is also an art of synthesis, of pulling together, encompassing other design activities as well as itself experimenting with new ones.

This year the course unfolds some of these phenomena - through the projects that each of the Architectural Design Studios (ADS) have set, through this year's college-wide lecture series, 'cybaroque', and through generally softening the way the course works.

Nigel Coates
Professor of Architectural Design
Course Director of Architecture and Interiors

'Architectural discourse
is experienced inattentively,
in the same way in which
we experience the discourse
of movies or television,
the comics or advertising.'

Umberto Eco
on mass appeal in architecture

Alphaville

October 97

We kick off with a project called Alphafile. Based on the 1965 Godard movie **Alphaville**, a cult movie which posits a totalitarian society controlled by a single artificial intelligence called Alpha 60. Love and emotion are considered a crime punishable by execution. Neither fascist nor communist, it raises questions as to the outcome of society saturated by communication to the point of living in the advert. Shot completely in black and white, and in carefully chosen locations in Paris, it builds a parallel world that cleverly converts the world we know. In fact it uses exactly the strategy we tend to use as architects - to build the hypothetical by reassembling what we know, edging towards freedom.

I thought the students were going to be bored by the film, because it is a bit long-winded, a bit stilted. Yet everyone was into it in no time. The proposition was this: if Alphaville was to be remade now, and shot in London, how would it be? We asked first years to study the film and rescript five of the key scenes. "So get out there, look at the city as a film maker would, read the spirit of buildings but convert their meaning, turn them upside down if you can."
The Barbican featured heavily in the work, its tunnels, its towers, its grim dystopic alienation overwhelming its rather heavy-handed Metabolist intentions. Lots of models, lots of movies. We seemed to be off on the right foot.

Meanwhile there's a trip to the Dome, now with its masts ready to be hauled into position. What exactly does the Greenwich site promise more than sheer size? We take a ride along the Docklands light railway trundling past Canary Wharf, past all the cute 80s re-con village stations and we get off at Gallions Reach for the wasteland that was used as the set for Kubrick's Full Metal Jacket. Old plant has been heaved by giants out of the ground to look like massive cannons in a lunar landscape. Demolition is underway - in a few weeks the scene will be gone without trace. Big issues are implied by the contrast of this sort of pathos, and all the urban aspirations these trigger, against the celebratory and similarly overscaled backdrop of the Dome....

John Thackara opens this year's major lecture series 'cybaroque' with 'lost in space - a travellers tale': he posits air space as an invisible yet all-pervasive spatial organisation greater than any single architecture. Virtual yet hyperreal, he lays the ground for the whole issue of the sensual space between reality and virtuality intended by '**cybaroque**'. Touches of Alphaville here too.

NIGEL COATES
Professor of Architectural Design
Course Director of Architecture and Interiors
Partner at Branson Coates Architecture

Alphafile is followed by presentations by each of the ADS's outlining their themes for the year. ADS1 is taking up the space between the real and the virtual. ADS2 will concentrate on accumulative urban development by focusing on the London rail termini as potential metropolitan conditions in themselves. ADS3 wants to parallel the expo phenomenon now firmly linked to the millennium and more particularly to the Dome. Piers Gough architalks about approaching practice with a pleasure principle not seen since Piranesi; Oliver Solway of Softroom blasts us with a range of real dreams in the form of finely crafted form-Z's of products and spaces of the (Wallpaper) future.

November 97
The ADS's are well under way with their first cycle of research projects. ADS1 is looking at Web cam sites - Internet pages where the host has a camera permanently set up at home. A range of sites provide virtual windows into intangible but real worlds, which by virtue of the frame can generate elaborate hypothetical constructs of what these spaces are actually like.

ADS2 has been out charting the terrain through and around the major rail termini of London. The sort of material documenting of these places enables the dynamic, activity and spirit driven side of the city to come through, and be available to work into strategies.

I try the first of a new think-tank format in which I get all the students of one year together. In the first I choose a snip of Kathy Acker's Bodies of Work, in which she portrays creative drive as a phallocentric illusion. What exactly is real creativity we ask? I am surprised that there is no strong resentment towards men continuing to hold on to the reins of power.

Ron Arad cybaroque: 'sports, science & artists' impressions'... very much impressions, because he decides not to do a conventional lecture, but to open the responsibility for the discussion to the audience. 'This is a question and answer session only - who wants to start?' But he is more than prepared, with a computer CD-ROM set-up that means that he can travel as quick as a click to illustrate his answer. Overwhelming situations of new furniture, products, his Tel Aviv interior and the house (maybe) to be in Hampstead.

Architectural agenda is full on for FAT, whose architalk puts forward project after project balanced between art and architectural practice. Their estate agents' project enabled the occupants of a whole street to choose artworks to be displayed on the usual sales boards outside their homes. While their projects for nightclubs such as the Leisure Lounge and their

diary_05

John Thackara

Ron Arad

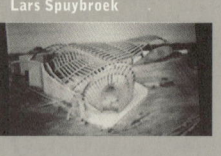

Lars Spuybroek

club in Swindon, systematise their spaces into a series of shock juxtapositions of larger than life references to the world of advertising, toys, potting sheds and other popular dreams.

In ADS2 Olivier Védrine cajoles everyone into a rapid series of labworks with his Body, Mind, Psycho series of one day projects. The Psycho one gives each person a chance to lie on the psychiatrist's couch in a tent specially built in the corner of the studio. "What is your dream architecture?" Have sex and architecture got anything to do with one another? Big questions.

December 97

Judit Kimpian has secured funding for her research work into new inflatable form. Growing out of her MA work for a series of portable buildings, she is now pursuing the possibility of air structures with a double helix primary structure. The German company Festo supports and encourages. Buro Happold provide the know-how and computer modelling.

At the end of term crits each ADS presents its own cycle of research set up by their autumn projects. We're now trying to hold crits simultaneously for each of the ADS's, in the tank, the bridge, and the seminar room. Lots of incisive work that tackles the ADS agendas with nouse and invention. In ADS1 I particularly like Mei Ling's explorations of the cross over between the culture of the supermarket and Portobello market. She compares their products, she follows shoppers, eventually proposing a mobile Sainsbury's cabin that can nest between other stalls on Portobello Road.

January 98

Big change to the space on the 8th floor. The computer room has moved to the bridge, and my room has engulfed the old one. At last I'm not in a cupboard, and there's room to get a dozen people around the table.

Now's the time to write the brief, and we've asked everyone to write 500 words and pin them all up in the Gallery. Most are as vague as possible. We complain that sites are only approximate, no definitive programme, no areas - but there is edge in some, others need to be developed. But the seeds are there.

Lars Spuybroek delivers cybaroque 4. His focus is H^2O, his freshwater pavilion on a beach in the south of Holland. Like a metallic beached whale from the outside, inside swirls and responds to the combined forces of the water and the visitor. Creative neurons activated by his truly liquid architecture.

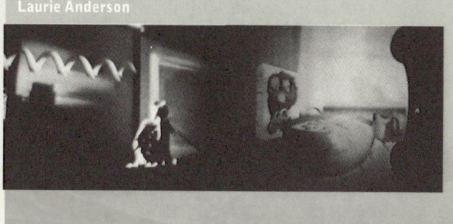

Laurie Anderson

Lots of little plastic creatures and people appearing in the work, lots of photos, lots of form-Z. Several of the projects are layered organic, with walls butting up against fruit shapes that look as though they could never stand up... waves of chat about connection (or disjunction) between form and programme.

February 98

Nigel's second year think-tank: what do each of us think we're up to? What hormones are we trying to release into architecture? 'to stay in the future, but frequent the present... there are no females/males, we are all individuals... brains with extrapolations' (John B); 'not a desire to be heroic but... an injection of heroism' (Esther W); 'understanding complexity, working with the interdisciplinary and creating a balance for the body could enrich perception' (Julia T); ''I'm a lifestyle suggestor and hip hop is the best music to suggest a lifestyle' (Peter M) ''to edit the environment down to its bare essentials but for that environment to be the richest place, most full of life' (Richard B); 'I would like to think that my work could have a part of my being when I was three years old and a part of my being at 30, 40, 50, 60, 100...' (Silvia T).

Cybaroque 5: **Laurie Anderson** packs them in to the Royal Geographical Society lecture theatre. She's set up slide, projection and sound equipment on the stage, and then drifts through a series of stories with a psychospatial undertow... art projects she'd like to do, ones she has done and her new project to stage Moby Dick as an opera. The audience is intrigued, seduced, sometimes lost but always with her. Between virtuality and reality, for her architecture is a cultural desire. Then, back to the College for the Architecture Interiors & Furniture Interim Show. Lots of models, lots of moving images, lots of invention and a real take on architecture as a cultural condition. Several of the exhibits are working sophisticated ideas in with a toylike expression, with Britain's models. Some of the furniture students have done portacabins, which look more conventionally architectural than anything we've done, but this sort of volte-face is what the College should be more about, about trying on each other's shoes.

diary_07

Christian Möller

Light Surgeons

March 98

Christian Möller, interactive architect from Frankfurt delivers a pocket history of real life projects that harness physical and electronic media. Most of these focus on interactivity in public spaces, combining sound and moving images that swap the scale of the building and the body. Lots of influence, with sound and light pieces appearing in studio projects.

End of term crits reveal projects which, though unfinished, have a certain architectural materiality. The sense of the three ADS's activities really seem to support one another.

The **Bilbao trip**, where the texture of a decaying industrial port crosses with gleaming new projects, like diamonds in a colander. Lots of mad group photos with wavy titanium sails in the background. Fiona and Knut succeed in getting the students to investigate the contrasting textures of the city by plotting lines extending from the bridges over the river. Some nice drawings brought back as souvenirs.

April 98

First years dive into the **one2one** with the usual panic at the thought of actually making a full size part of a building in two weeks. When it comes to the day, and the running order set, we begin in Howie Street with Johann's jelly igloo - a prototype for his architectural 'entity' at the heart of London Bridge Station. Mark follows with a pop-up bootleg stall which, like a fairground sideshow, can be quickly erected and open for business in a matter of seconds. Karen solicits Johann into performing her piece - a balcony that responds to a 'domestic' by dividing into two spaces as long as the row continues.

Up at Kensington Gore the rest of the first years have colonised various parts of the building with full-scale mock ups of parts of their projects, including Nirpal's wax wall, Mei Ling's tilting stair, Alasdair's crash device, and Nicola's rubber performance wall. Best one2one yet.

Tyler Brûlé's talk on the inside story at Wallpaper magazine fills the seminar room.

May 98

The **Light Surgeons** fill the seminar room with five movie projects, three slide projectors and lots of music. Sharp shapes and medical diagrams over action loops, throbbing text and the hallucinogenic city.

Cybaroque 8: Zaha Hadid ends the series with a blast of a talk articulated around artificial nature, and the manipulation of the landscape plane. Image after image of split, saturated, cleaved surfaces builds up an architectural vision that combines freedom with strategy. Projects like the MIT superplan build up a complexity which is infinitely expansive (she never seems to stay within her site), and engages a sense of being there unlike the work of so many architects, you can sense what it might be like to be there, if even in the mind...

Final crits show that despite each of the ADS's starting out with a diverse range of issues, there is a remarkable confluence between their eventual outcomes. We talk about making a big model of all the graduating projects together. Though ranging in scale from the small multi-site adjustments of ADS1 to the major urban manoeuvres of ADS2, an underlying spirit seeks out a radical evolution of the city as we know it, not to some distant moment of the perfect state, but more as the late twentieth century sci-fi movie has shown, to a resonant expansion on the present.

June 98

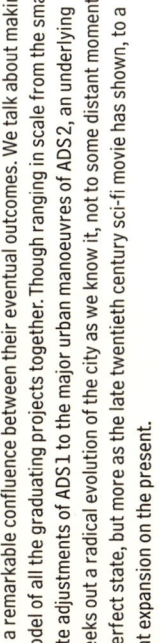

Zaha Hadid

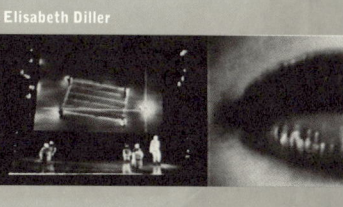

Elisabeth Diller

We're talking a gaudy star burst of carpet for the summer show, with a model in the foreground that puts the work of all the thesis projects together. Certainly there will be a scale problem with this model, with some of the ADS1 projects being a fraction of the size of other projects. But we've opted for the model as sign rather than truth. The model is intended to show what we had always hoped from the work of the year: that we're in the business of architecture as metropolitan culture that posits radical evolution, that reacts to what is around it, that spars off its many conditions. Far from engaging in some sort of master planning exercise, the work indicates a responsive and reactive way to the city evolving, a cross between ecology and futurology.

Having begun projects from the particular spatial (or transspatial) conditions of the Web, students in ADS1 have gradually translated these into physical space that in turn creates windows back towards the data world. By working around the term 'boudoir', notions of domesticity have found new transterritorial manifestations that explore the intimate condition of the body in the city as well as the bedroom. Chris's urban love triangle (page 23) results in an underground housing scheme for would-be triangles. Will's project (page 21) enhances the relationship between the home and the high street, with a chip shop that anticipates your order, and then expands this principle to three East London sites.

diary_09

Bilbao illustration

Amy takes up with the courier bikers of London (page 25) to devise a network of newsagents as base camps for local radio operated by the bikers themselves. Esther (page 29) has also been working with the home: she selects two contrasting Web cam sites - a man called Robert who lives in a neat suburban home, with the camera permanently trained on a parlour in which nothing much seems to happen, and the other one, Tori, a homecat who likes exhibiting herself in front of the camera as it scans back and forth. Both have provided models from which a hypothetical flat could be constructed, which results in a housing complex built on the Robert and Tori types. Juliet (page 27) takes a vast disused railway viaduct near Brick Lane as the focus of a number of other sites around London to reflect the city's multiculture. She assembles these into a sequence of public spaces, from pool to theatre, from marketplace to changing room. The resulting above- and-below park reconfigures its paths according to a range of triggers, such as the call to prayers, or the passing of traffic.

In ADS2 Julia (page 39) also occupies the airspace above a railway viaduct, this time in Southwark. Within a double helix structure, she builds a multilevel urban condition which houses a marketplace of office work. Chains of cabins front on to loose spaces for distraction as well as meeting. Routes through it constantly dip and dive to engender an ever-evolving choreography. Costas (page 41) infuses Euston with a shimmering meditation and fitness liquid architecture that floats above the existing concourse structures. Peter (page 37) makes the brave move of demolishing Euston's existing concourse and opens all of its functions out into the square to make a space which is both information saturated and yet free enough to be part of the city as a whole.

ADS3's series of workshops on British characteristics and institutions has resulted in a strong set of projects for Expo pavilions around London. Though Silvia's bridge pavilion (page 57) is near the Dome, others take up sites as far apart as Leicester Square and the South Bank. John's South Bank farm (page 51) uses the agrarian calendar and farming processes like sheering and muck spreading to set up a series of tools that can be applied to urban space. So his pavilion is a fluid 'rural' space that renders the existing foyers of the Festival Hall and the river terraces one continuous landscape of ever-shifting events. Richard's traffic incident (page 49) on the trunk road up to the Dome latches on to the existing scene of a Tudor Bethen pub sitting bang up against a gasometer. He extends this into a drive- as well as walk-through event that contrasts clues of a hypothetical crime

with enlarged devices of surveillance. Bruce (page 59), on the other hand makes use of the disused Dalston railway viaduct as a horse race track running from Broadgate to Hackney. While a giant horse's head forms the mouth to the race, a series of gardens and stands along the way combine the culture of the race meet with the cultural setting of east London. Dominic's lottery winners' finishing school and dogs home (page 55) occupies an overtly upmarket site just behind Bond Street. Side by side, the homes for charm school and the dogs parallel one another not least in architectural style. Both sample from classical and modernist pattern books, Robert Adam meets Corb. Dan's global meridian celebration (page 53) sites 24 identical telematic installations, one in each of the 24 time zones around the world. People at any one of these cannot only communicate directly with participants anywhere, but will get a strong sense of the position of the sun at any moment - day in New York means night in Beijing. Silvia's lan(d)guage bridge (page 57) is the most ambitious of these projects, with a giant structure that spans the Thames along the Meridian line. Based on the Braille system of touch reading, her design generates complex sequences and pools of space along the major beam of the bridge. Each of these exhibits a lexicon of language phenomena, from football to slang, from weaponry to graffiti.

We reckon it has been a good year with real cultures beginning to form in each of the studios. But more important than that, the work of each can add to the work of the others to generate a wider urban vision that anticipates the new interdisciplinary position of architecture. The intangible is in the air, but real people are there too. There is a real ydesire for the expression of design to connect with the ordinary and the incidental, with the city often being looked at so closely, so intimately, that many previously unseen hooks to the real have been found. We're exploring architecture as a new synthetic culture that overturns its product as fetishised function into part of the flow of city experience. Nothing to hide behind, just the enabler of self-awareness, all of which adds up to ∞-ville, a kind of hyper-post modernity, in which systems, processes and desires emerge as radical, iconic reconfigurations of the world we all know.

diary_11

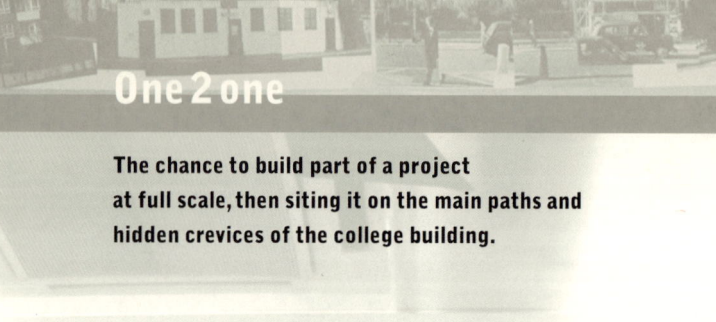

One 2 one

The chance to build part of a project at full scale, then siting it on the main paths and hidden crevices of the college building.

One2one student project

Architectural Design Studios

ADS1 boudoir borders - the virtual and real 'boudoir', at home and on the street, with multiple vision on multiple sites

ADS2 liquid states, hypernodes - expanding the metropolitan condition of London's rail termini, urban programmes highjacking the business of travel

ADS3 expo(se): Autobiography of a Nation - the 'other' Millennium - expo pavilions across London revealing British character traits

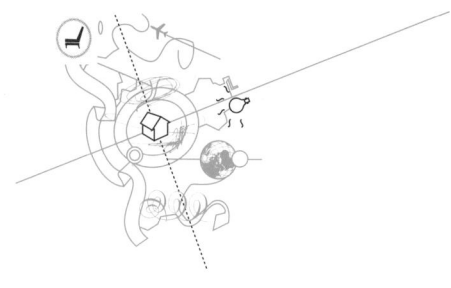

ADS ONE

boudoir borders

Robert Barker: 'Identity office'

THE CORPORATE ASSIGNED AVATARS EXPLORE THE VIRTUAL OFFICE PARK

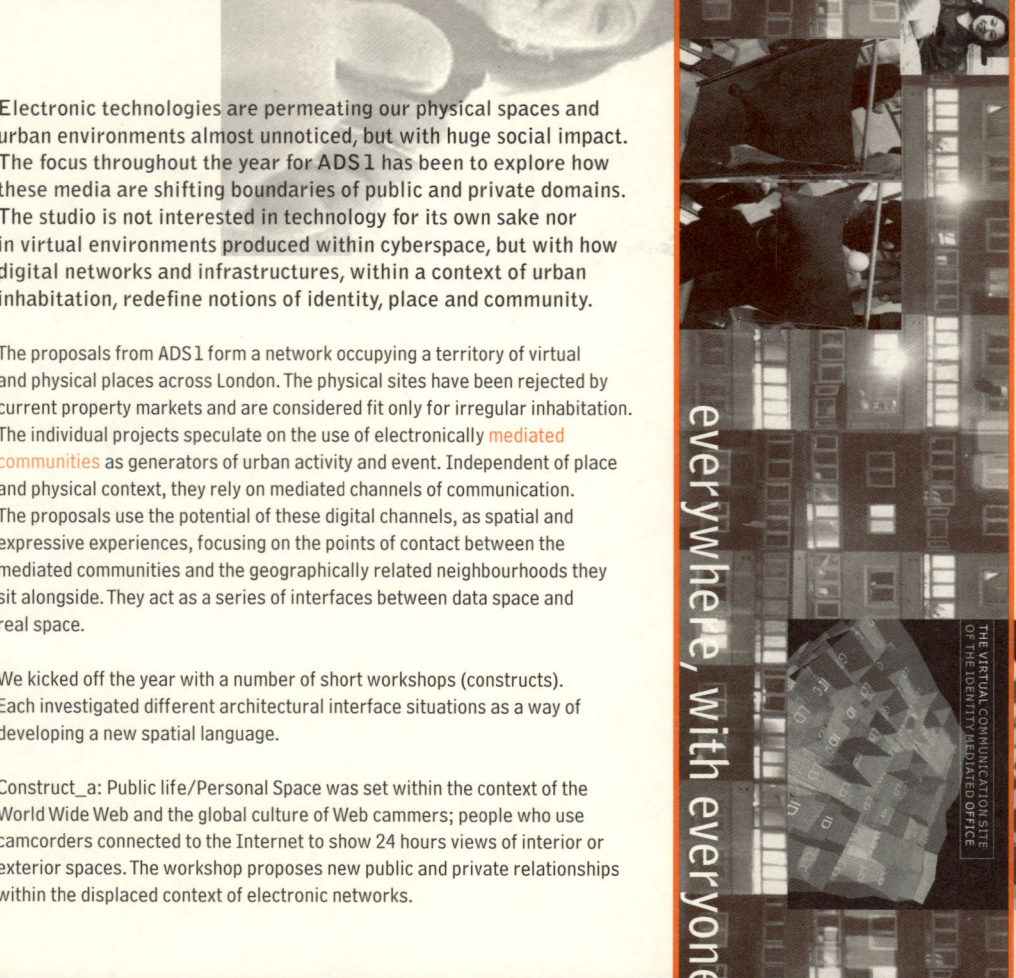

Nicola Girolami: 'Big fist', 'Fight', big image: 'Council block'

THE VIRTUAL COMMUNICATION SITE OF THE IDENTITY MEDIATED OFFICE

everywhere, with everyone

Electronic technologies are permeating our physical spaces and urban environments almost unnoticed, but with huge social impact. The focus throughout the year for ADS1 has been to explore how these media are shifting boundaries of public and private domains. The studio is not interested in technology for its own sake nor in virtual environments produced within cyberspace, but with how digital networks and infrastructures, within a context of urban inhabitation, redefine notions of identity, place and community.

The proposals from ADS1 form a network occupying a territory of virtual and physical places across London. The physical sites have been rejected by current property markets and are considered fit only for irregular inhabitation. The individual projects speculate on the use of electronically mediated communities as generators of urban activity and event. Independent of place and physical context, they rely on mediated channels of communication. The proposals use the potential of these digital channels, as spatial and expressive experiences, focusing on the points of contact between the mediated communities and the geographically related neighbourhoods they sit alongside. They act as a series of interfaces between data space and real space.

We kicked off the year with a number of short workshops (constructs). Each investigated different architectural interface situations as a way of developing a new spatial language.

Construct_a: Public life/Personal Space was set within the context of the World Wide Web and the global culture of Web cammers; people who use camcorders connected to the Internet to show 24 hours views of interior or exterior spaces. The workshop proposes new public and private relationships within the displaced context of electronic networks.

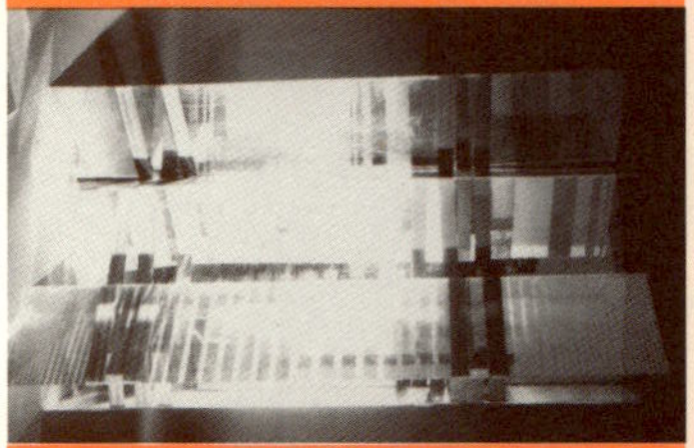

Cassion Castle: 'Cruciform', 'One 2 one', top: 'Telepresence: Garden alotement'

KNUT HOVLAND
AA Dipl, email: flipsite@online.no
tutor of ADS 1

FIONA RABY
MA RCA (ARCH), MPhil RCA (CRD)
tutor of ADS 1

one to one

Nicola immediately logged on to an overweight girl and her bedroom camsite. Her public identity was digitally manipulated by stretching images of herself and her friends, creating a simulated identity through the medium. Nicola took these controlled conditions and re-located them into the urban setting of two high-rise council estates in Battersea. The girl controls her appearance both physically and virtually. On the Net she presents herself in a Hello magazine style and manipulates images of herself in a thin stretched reality. A fridgecam initiated and controlled by opening and closing the fridge door, reveals her unchilled relationship to food. This action publishes images of herself peering into her fridge across the physical facade of the housing estate. Nicola proposes a similar system of visual interaction for all of the residents to break the anonymity of the estate.

Uninspired with views of dark bedrooms across the Atlantic, Cassion, on-line, back in London, hypothetically constructed a transparent neighbourhood. The global nature of Web cams suggest a state of omnipresence and anonymity. Socialise this space by adding proximity and identity and the rules completely change. Cassion speculated on the visual relationship of four Web cammers housed in a physical cruciform unit. The forced proximity, although still virtual, eroded their anonymity, changing the boundary condition. Public and private become redefined through varying degrees of visual permeability, the physicality of solid walls, different time zones, the light controlled transparency of two-way mirrors and the digital territory of four cams and monitors.

The blatant visual directness of the average Web cammer set Rebecca off on an instant tangent. Not convinced by its primitive social communication, she proposed an alternative construct based on collective sleeping. She identified the potential for sensual connectivity through the safety of a medium. This enhanced remote experience of other sleeping bodies was constructed around a series of physically distant bedrooms and connected through a series of abstract electronic devices. The telepresent sensitivity of your sleeping partner(s) was reduced to heat exchange, subtle movements in sleeping, furniture and ambient lighting.

ADS 1_17

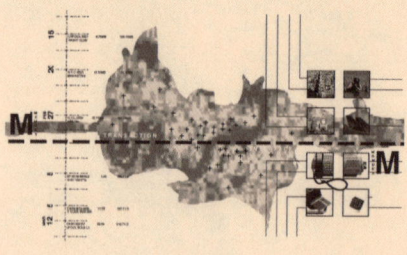

Karen Adcock: one2one, four stages of 'having a domestic' dispute_separation_negotiation_reconciliation.

Charlotte Boyens: 'Memorybank'

'always, forever, now' damien hirst

Construct_a investigated the public and private territories of a private domain, with the possibility of total personal control of the physical and virtual boundaries. In Construct_b (Transaction Interface) we considered the public domain; an urban situation with little or no personal control. The shop window can be described as the seam between the street and the shop, a physical space representing the transaction between lifestyle, objects and electronic information.

Chris (page 22) hi-jacked three camera transmission points, at three different scales for the potential sale of information. On the local 'shop window' scale he positioned himself, wearing a small 'body noticeboard' within the view of a security camera transmitting internally within the building. His second point offered a 'local space' for global sale on the Internet. Wearing a larger sandwich body-ad, he positioned himself on a seat within the Web cam gaze of a central London cafe. His urban site for global intervention was the football stadium. With the help of the crowd he occupied a free ad-space in a national TV transmission through a double-sided banner. These actions managed to position the designer as an active participant within large commercial networked data systems. He manipulated the electronic media by strategic positioning and timely scheduling. This direct action also identified the essential individual control needed within larger electronic infrastructures to achieve the ubiquitous inhabitation of his Urban Love Triangle.

The electronic, social and physical components identified in these initial constructs set up a potential architectural language for the constructed network in the second term. Although the studies were small in scale and self-contained, they were complex and rich enough to form the basis of the main programme. Once placed within our network of sites, most effort went into understanding and articulating the space in-between the virtual and physical. The one week workshop with Carlos Villanueva-Brandt in February was a difficult session for most, but fruitful for the committed.

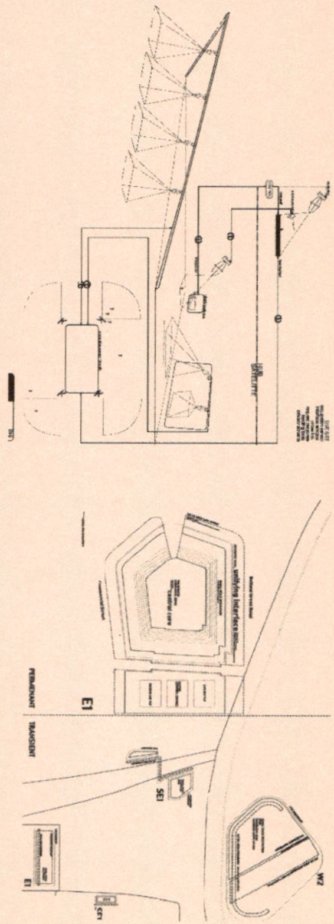

Kirsteen Mackay: 'Memobank', livesite and physical

Mei-Ling Juan: '12 red squares'

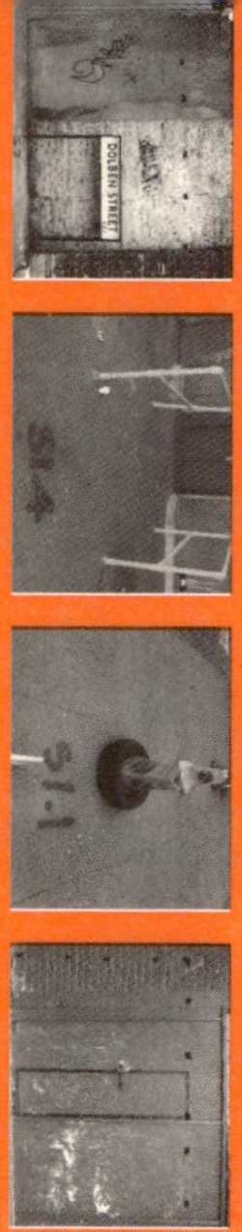

Karen Adcock
Robert Barker
Charlotte Boyens
Cassion Castle
Will Deakins
Chris Donoghue
Nicola Girolami
Mei-Ling Juan
Kirsteen Mackay
Amy Nicholson
Juliet Spartinos
Rebecca Vincent
Esther Waterfield

Kirsteen produced a beautiful pair of drawings outlining the physical proximity of her proposed art institution in relationship to its urban satellite exhibition sites. Her wire diagram specified the virtual administration of past, present and future art production accommodating the individual's points of control and choice within the individual exhibition spaces.

Fiction, continuity of experience and points of control have become key spatial elements in the ADS1 network of proposals.

Esther (page 29) proposes to construct a new housing estate modelled on the characteristics of two very different webcammers, Tori and Robert. Tori uses a moving camera to reveal her body from every angle while she masturbates, while, what appears to be an uneventful view of a large banal sofa in Robert´s living room, reveals a new space behind the sofa, a place we cannot see, but can start to imagine; a space of fiction. Two modular units, one based on a 'Tori' apartment and one on a 'Robert', form a new programming of public and private space, assembled into two mixed housing blocks. The void between them exist as a potential space of fiction and collective communication.

Karen proposes a domestic interior that provides a space of refuge both within the family unit and within the community. Electronic gadgets and domestic objects are customised and assembled as points of control to provide spaces of negotiation and to act as interfaces for reconciliation. These points of control locate the virtual within physical space.

Will's (page 21) proposal occupies 3 sites in London. Although his 'home' is physically fragmented, the separated domestic elements and events are brought together through electronic connections and inter-relationships. The abstract lighting of a church in the centre of the sleeping accommodation in Peckham is connected to fridge activity in an urban lounge in Southwark, and to individual food compositions selected from an electronic ingredients list in the dining room off Brick Lane in the East. The urban domesticity of this collapsed home exist as a continuous experience rather than a nostalgic point of reference.

ADS1_19

age : years **'Urban lounge'**, living room model

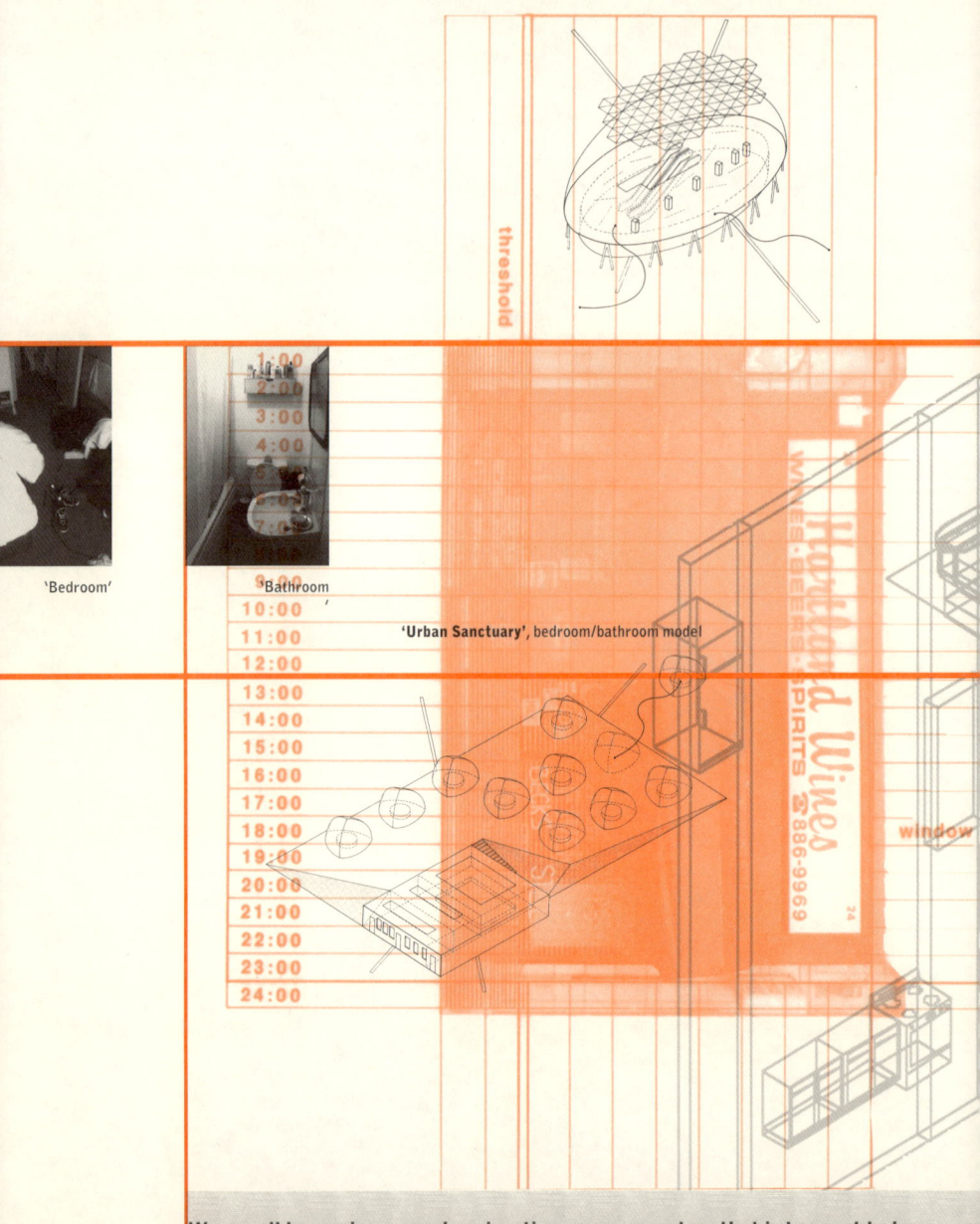

threshold

'Bedroom'

Bathroom

1:00
2:00
3:00
4:00
5:00
6:00
7:00
8:00
9:00
10:00
11:00
12:00
13:00
14:00
15:00
16:00
17:00
18:00
19:00
20:00
21:00
22:00
23:00
24:00

'Urban Sanctuary', bedroom/bathroom model

window

'We are all becoming nomads, migrating across a system that is too vast to be our own, but in which we are fully involved, translating and transforming bits and elements into local instances of sense. It is this remaking, this transmutation, that makes such texts and languages - the city, cinema, music, culture and the contemporary world - habitable: as though they were a space borrowed for a moment by a transient, an immigrant, a nomad.' Iain Chambers, Cities without maps

'Virtual home Public life/personal space', background 'Urban dining', kitchen model

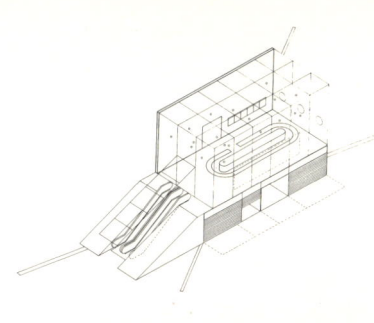

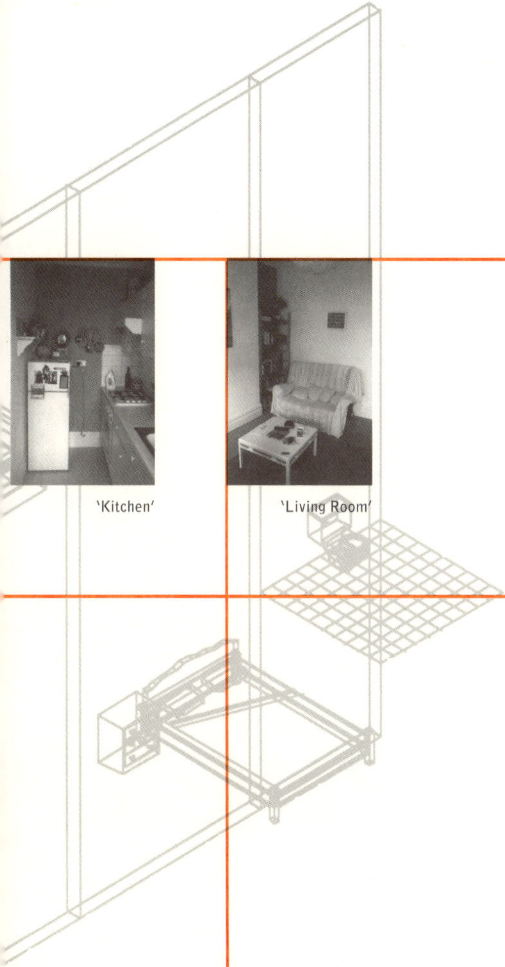

'Kitchen'   'Living Room'

William Deakins
MA in Architecture and Interiors: RCA
BA in ID: Middlesex University

Domestic space is dispersed throughout the city; Home is no longer a singular place but a collective of personal spaces, each components of our individual boudoir.

This project proposes a networked community of three geographically distanced domestic environments; Electronic and communication technologies connect the physically distanced sites allowing for a sensorily accelerated urban domesticity.

The lives of six clients were documented through urban diaries, with each diarist noting location, situation and incidental events every hour over a one week period. Spatial and social situations acquired through the diaries were used as a model for the occupation of uninhabited urban sites, each a Set for an alternative programme of domestic enactment.

SET_1: Southwark_Living Room\Door
SET_2: Bermondsey_Bedroom\Bathroom
SET_3: Spitalfields_Kitchen\Fridge

COLLECTIVE BOUDOIR

urban love triangle
ONE DAY WE WILL ALL LIVE THIS WAY

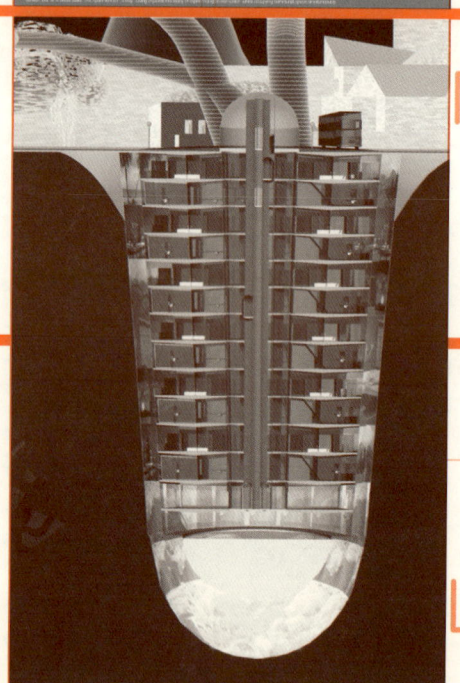

'Apartment for "three-way" living'

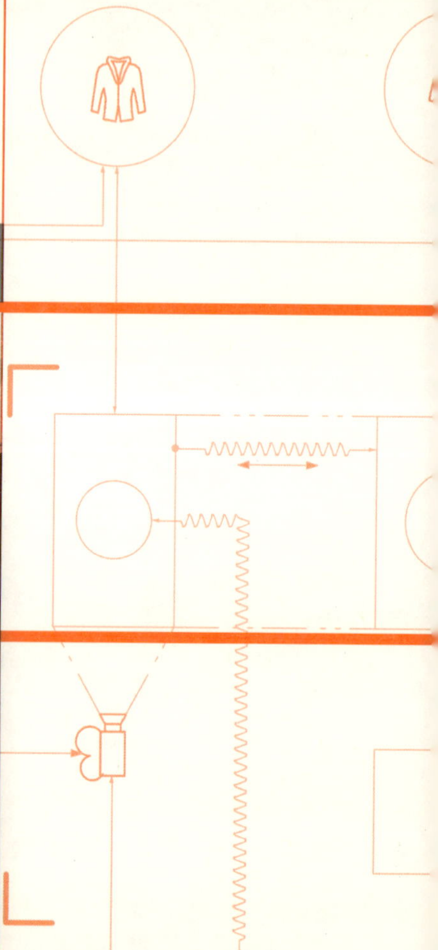

boudoir ('bu:dwa:, -dwc:) n.
a woman's bedroom or a private sitting room.
The Collins Paperback English Dictionary - 1996

Web cam ('survl:an-ce, ca|mera:) n.
1) an electronic camera connected to the World Wide Web
2) a device to relay 'Live' images taken from the source camera to the screen of any Internet browser
Still to be officially defined - 1998

URBAN LOVE TRIANGLE:
Three-way Living

Christopher Donoghue

MA in Architecture and Interiors: RCA
BA in AR: Kingston University

The aim of my project is to translate the ever flourishing virtual network between 'Web cam' users across the globe into a physical relationship. The resultant physical spaces will speculate on the potential interface between the public and private domain, utilising controlling devices implemented by the Internet for 'Web cam' browsers.

The project began with a story of three characters; the Husband, the Wife and the Mistress. Each character occupied their own 'boudoir' which either physically or virtually overlapped the others. These relationships set out a series of new physical spaces which would function as a network within an urban context, but at a virtual scale. The Apartment for 'three-way' Living explores this reality of experiencing private space whilst occupying communal space simultaneously.

Hijacking the system
'Chest ad', 'Full sandwich', '!Double Whammy'

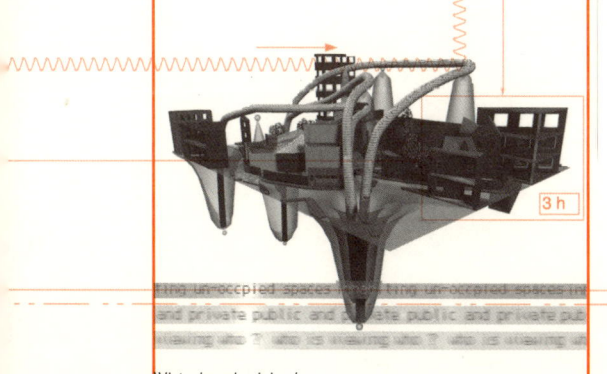

'Virtual condominium'

RADIO COURIER

'Views from motorcycle courier's camera'

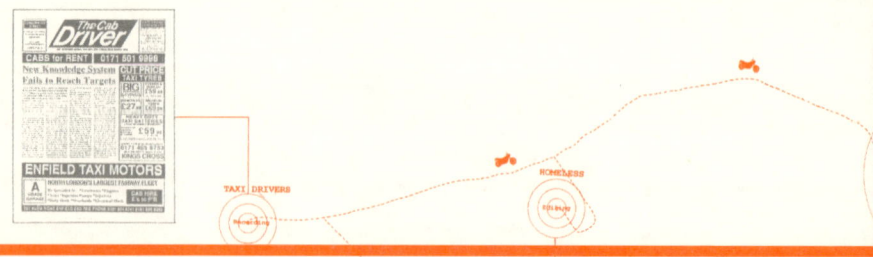

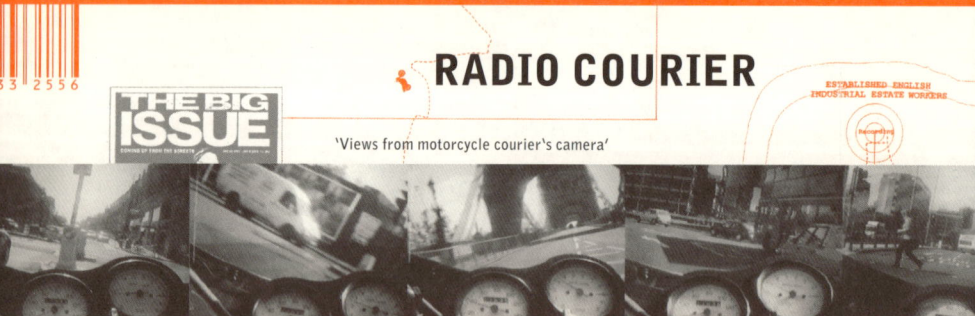

'The offices the girl rode between were electronically continuous - in effect, a single desktop, the map of distances obliterated by the seamlessness and instantaneous nature of communication. Yet this very seamlessness which had rendered physical mail an expensive novelty and as such created the need for the service the girl provided.'

Extract from William Gibson's 'Virtual Light'

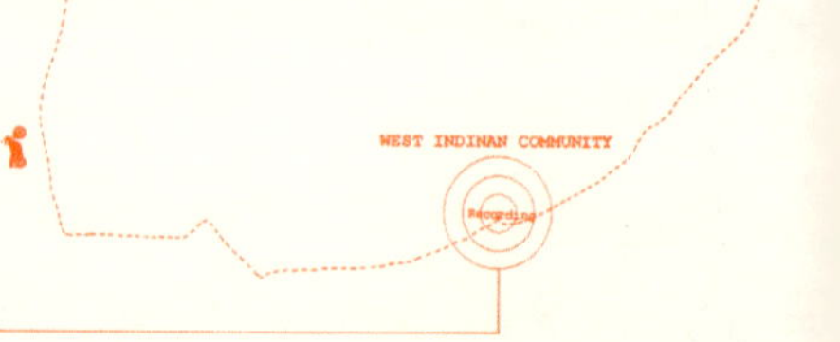

'Radio courier network'

'Zaeen News Security Camera'

Amy Nicholson
MA in Architecture and Interiors: RCA
BA in AR: Oxford Brookes University

In an age of increasingly paperless communication, the motorcycle courier has an expanding role in the transportation of physically precious information. Couriers on a daily basis risk their lives skilfully weaving through London's grimy and congested road network, yet they are placeless and little respected by those they serve.

My proposal is to transfer the courier into a new framework and architecture that welcomes and utilises his unique understanding of the city. The aim is to connect ten fragmented communities within London via a mobile voice-based radio station. The courier provides the physical and electronic link, travelling on a timetabled circuit to a newsagent in each of the culturally diverse communities. He conducts live interviews covering topical local issues and debates that are relayed live to the other newsagents on the network. The newsagents become a new community interface for the dissemination of local as well as national information.

The movements of the courier on his circuit are visually fed back to each newsagent from a camera fixed to the front of his motorbike and by tapping into security cameras on the road network and within the newsagents.

As with the Internet, rapid exchange of information and live events are made available to physically segregated spaces... but with physical experience.

ADS 1_25

'Plan physical and digital connections'

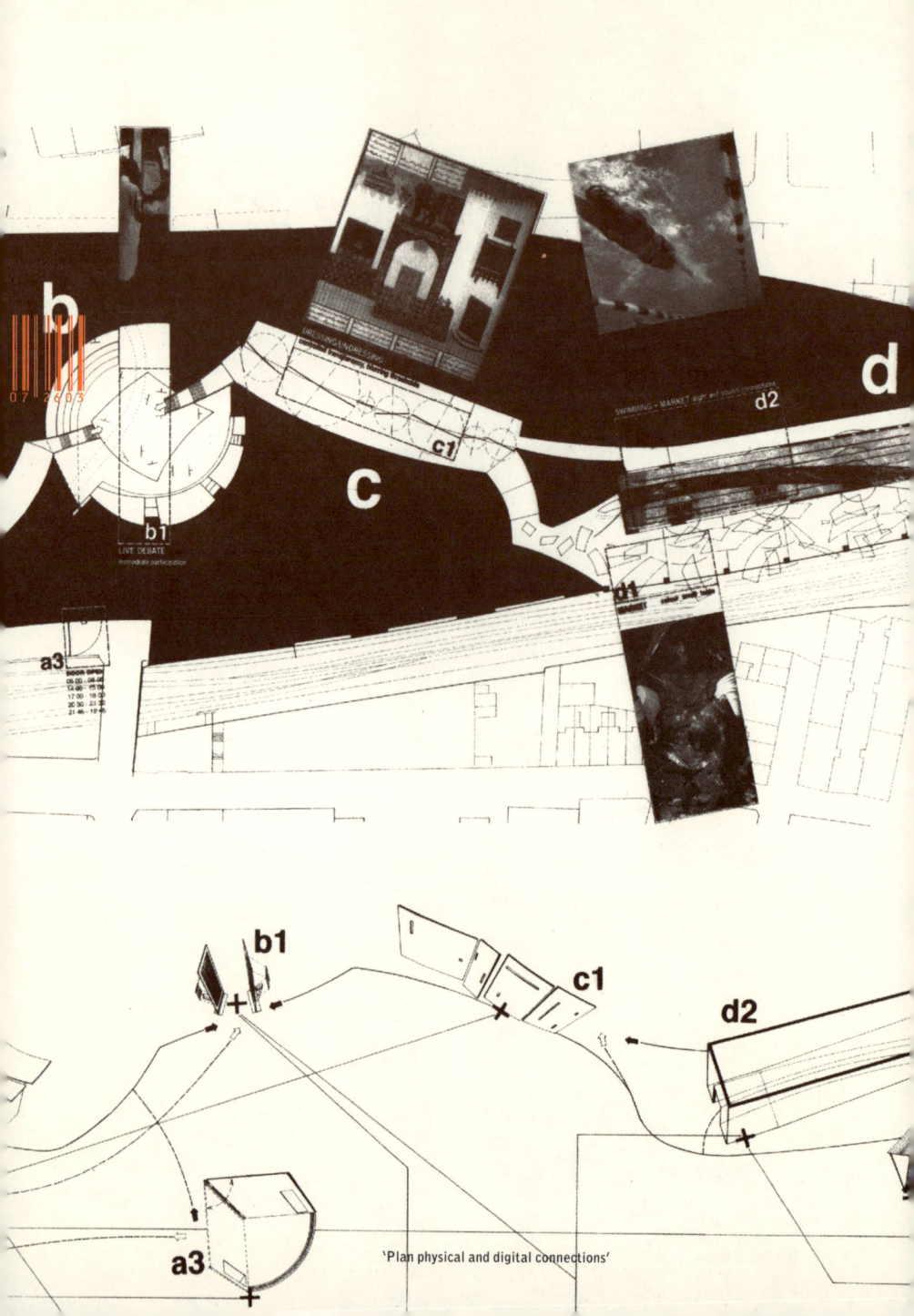

CULTURESCAPE
Urban wasteland as narrative

'Brick Lane'

Juliet Spartinos
MA in Architecture and Interiors: RCA
BA in AR: Oxford Brookes University

I propose a new form of urban landscape as an alternative to the 'Englishness' of London's royal parks. It will enhance the rich diversity of London as a multicultural state, feeding off three diverse cultures/communities that inhabit very specific areas of London:

'Brixton market'

1_BRICK LANE_ Bengali
2_BRIXTON MARKET_ Afro Caribbean
3_EDGWARE ROAD_ Arab

The site sits in the heart of a politically sensitive area, as a result of migratory settlements. Formerly a railway goods yard, it now exists as a void, a nine acre plot of wasteland.

Agents within the three communities will be electronically linked to this site, providing experiential access routes up to the nine acre plateau. The landscape will function according to the timescape, event and social trends of these communities. This will physically communicate the merging of cultures within London and will provide incentive for the wasteland site to grow relatively to its surrounding socio-cultural conditions.

'Edgware Road'

'Robertcam'

'Robert living room'

'Mall'

'Robert camera'

MORE TEA, VICAR?
A block of flats for Web cam users
Jamaica Road, Bermondsey

'Tori meets Robert'

'Toricam'

'Tori living room'

Esther Waterfield
MA in Architecture and Interiors: RCA
BA in AR: University of North London

Tori and Robert are two Web cam users (found on the Internet) who have cameras in their living rooms. They both transmit images of their home lives to the Internet, making a part of their domestic domain public. I have recruited them to be the inhabitants of this housing proposal in Bermondsey.

Robert's camera has a fixed viewpoint which allows him and his family to get to the kitchen without being seen in their pyjamas. Tori's camera follows her around as she masturbates, rolling on and off the sofa.

I like the way that Robert displays his propriety and Tori displays her impropriety.

I have designed a block of flats to accommodate a community of Toris and Roberts. It is designed to play off the different ways that people display themselves to each other.

The project explores and celebrates notions of display and voyeurism, proposing an architecture which is about bay windows, shop windows, sofas, front gardens and the spaces in between.

I have called it 'More tea, Vicar?' because it suggests a kind of community and an afternoon tea setting but with a saucy undertone.

'Tori Camera'

'Terminal concourses
are the ramblas and agoras
of the future city, time free zones....
the transformation of Britain into
the ultimate departure lounge'
'Ballard'

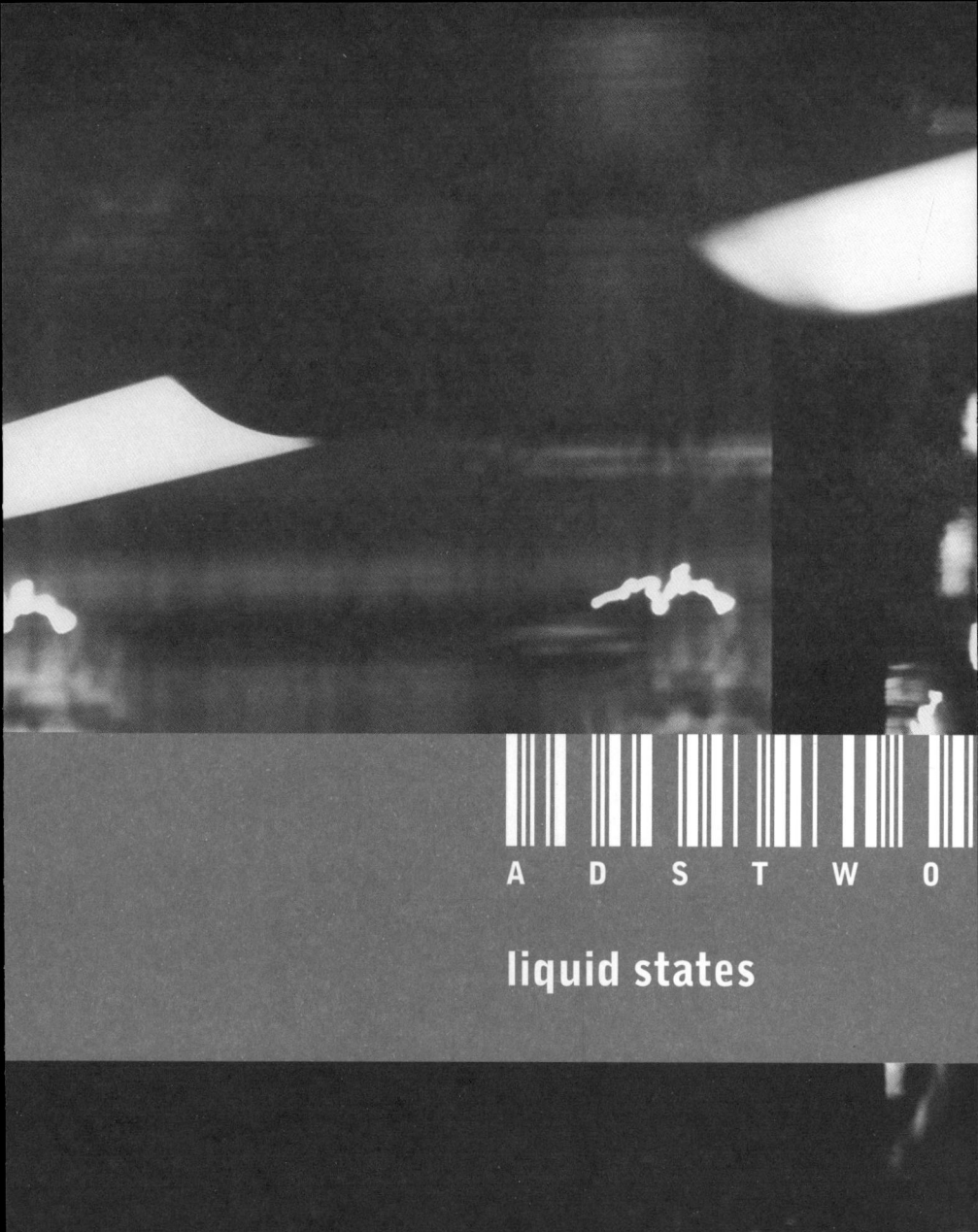

ADSTWO

liquid states

The scale and diversity of contemporary urban communications pose almost insurmountable problems and contradictions, with conventional boundaries of architectural design being too restrictive to fully address the myriad of related issues: transport, transience, telecommunications, disturbance, comfort, leisure, homelessness and changing patterns of work.

ADS2 sets out to develop the concept of 'urban infrastructure', engaging structures that allow metropolitan life to flourish and support the rapid change that characterises the contemporary city. We seek to broaden the definition of infrastructure to include the social and the cultural. Form does matter, but the essential aim is to examine design strategies for complex urban situations.

ADS2's projects focus on six major London rail termini, which form the city's key communication nodes. They are London's check-ins and conferencing suites but also offer a frenetic metropolitan experience.

We began by uncovering and mapping the diverse activities that coalesce in these places, from the exotic and the illegal to the mundane. These lead to propositions that encompass 'architecture as experience', 'materiality', 'connectivity', and the 'city as an interior landscape'.

The autumn term included a series of trips, talks and labworks to provide each person with the necessary insights and conceptual toolkits. Prepared with this, we set out to positively negotiate the city's myriad, dynamic forces.

Nirpal Bansal: '5 mins 3 secs'

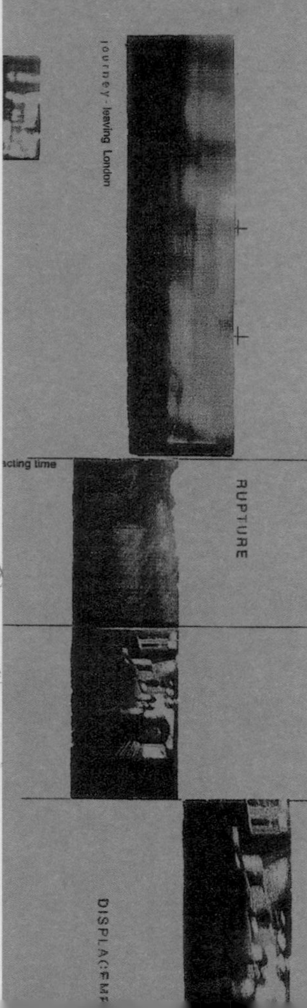

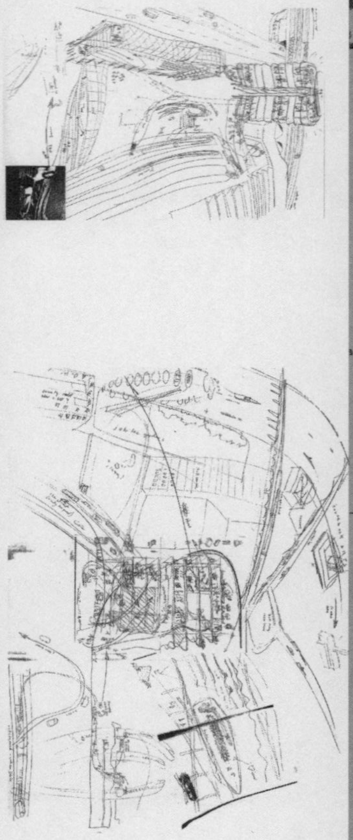

Carl Turner: 'The red carpet', two drawings

We firstly looked at movement and threshold through a series of 24 hour mapping exercises recording existing activities and connections. This led to various proposals for interventions that alter or 'rewire' the current situation. In Nirpal's project at Victoria, a filmic investigation of the commuter belt travel has been transposed into a hotel where to 'escape' from the city doesn't actually mean physically leaving it.

Far ranging sources were consulted by the ADS, from the Demos Report to leading London planners, including Fred Manson of Southwark and Westminster Council's Grahame King. Trips included a 'behind the scenes' visit to Alsop & Störmer's nearly completed North Greenwich underground station - a significant contemporary project that will provide the principal gateway to the Millennium Dome.

During our weekend trip to Paris, hosted by Olivier Védrine, we went snooping in the passages of the fabric district. We ventured backstage at the phenomenal Grand Bibliotèque, passed through the multilayered programme of Les Halles where public swimming pool and commerce happily co-exist. Passing out in the 'cross-programmed' Carmen Bar at 5am only to regroup for an early morning roll call at the slick white modernist mansion of Meier's Canal Plus HQ.

Throughout the year we encourage an experience-led exploration of the city. This approach was heightened by Olivier Védrine's labworks which explored architectural propositions from the mind-artificial nature, the body-materiality through to the psycho-reality and virtuality.

RAILWAY STATIONS MARK THE LIFE IN A BIG CITY, OVERFLOWING WITH EXCITEMENT BUT LACKING IN CONTRAST

JOHN F. SMITH
BA, DipArch, PhD(RCA), RIBA
tutor of ADS 2, John Smith Associates

ANDREW ONRAËT
MA(RCA), tutor of ADS 2
Urban salon

OLIVIER VÉDRINE
DipArch, tutor of ADS 2
Olivier Védrine: Designer Scénographe

Frank Amankwah: 'Welcome Deck'

ADS 2 **33**

A trip to Bilbao was inspirational; from the cool functionalism of Foster's underground system to Ghery's Guggenheim, where one building can act as a generator to the city.

Post-vacation, armed with tales of Spanish living, the spring term saw the many facets of the year's influences coming to the fore.

The year's projects successfully resist simplistic categorisation. Nevertheless, a series of themes is evident, tempered by individual responses to the particular social, cultural or physical conditions. Many projects are concerned with movement and transience: there is a recognition that these places represent a heightened experience of the impermanence of the inner city. There is also a desire to investigate the consequences of cross-programming.

Costas Tsangarakis's project (page 41) deals with Euston Station and uses a radical urban landscaping strategy to open up and revitalise a particularly banal terminal concourse. Peter Morris (page 37) subverts formulaic station design by removing the periphery of the station. A sensual, liquid, architectural language has been an undertone of some projects. Both London Bridge projects deal with the issues of urban density, but in quite different ways. Julia's new laced office platform (page 39) straddles the railway viaducts of Southwark. Johann carefully inserts poetic structures into the harsh environment of the existing station. On the other side of town at Paddington, Frank has developed a "Welcome Deck" that becomes both a 'gateway' and a connection point to and from London, acting on both the local and the international level: check-in at Paddington, next stop Rio.

Roberta Grassi: 'Urban Boudoir', Busstop

Johann Schnaus: left: 'Also available in lime flavour'
right: 'Excavating London Bridge'

Carl Turner critically examines the isolation of the Eurostar Terminal from its urban surroundings. He lays out a metaphorical red carpet by identifying an 'undiscovered' public space to be given an energetic re-programming.

Francesca Gernone pursues a creative reinterpretation of the Great Western Hotel at Paddington, ripping out some earlier accretions and re-establishing a relationship with the station and the city. Roberta Grassi's work acts as a counter to the crass commercialisation of railway stations, developing proposals for Victoria that re-evaluate public space through the insertion of unexpected cultural experiences. Likewise John Senior and Barbara Hauer have chosen to support the various sub-cultures that inhabit the Kings Cross area, generating strategies that resist facile developers solutions. Throughout the year ADS2 projects have pursued an energetic cosmopolitan vision of London's future, envisaging a hybrid mix of overlapping activities and spatial experiences which embrace the diversity of urban life.

Frank Amankwah
Nirpal Bansal
Francesca Gernone
Roberta Grassi
Barbara Hauer
Gihan Karunaratne
Peter Morris
Johann Schnaus
John Senior
Julia Thomas
Costas Tsangarakis
Carl Turner

Francesca Gernone: 'Bubblewall'

John Senior: 'Sh*pping and Fucking'

ADS 2_35

Site: Euston Square, meet the city.

History: Euston has become a remote gap in the city fabric. The notion of any spatial interaction has become lost and isolated.

The relationship between the City and the Station has shifted from being considered as just a so-called gateway and a monument shed that is celebrating the Industrial Age, to becoming a place within the city, that has defined its own transient lfestyle.

Proposal:

1. Remove the existing buildings of Euston Station. Rewire the function of catching a train into Euston Square, as an urban performance, so that the traveller can catch a train by inhabiting the City rather than a station building.

2. To elaborate upon the distinct lifestyle that is now defined by the joining of any transport system and an urban environment. Redefining the Public Square. Secondary functions and the transient lifestyles that a station attracts now inhabits the surrounding buildings of Euston Square.

3. 'The public Square'- Three spaces (Time, Market and Public) will be integrated into the redefined of Euston Station becoming a public space.

'Time Square'- The performance of trains arriving and departing will be broken down into three periods - floating destinations, time in relation to the platform and the countdown to departure.

'Market Square'- Certain services will be provided within strategic locations of the square, to cater for the space to be commercially used and commercially determined.

'Public Square'- This is a piece of land that is given back to the public as a place of urban leisure, providing interaction via the square.

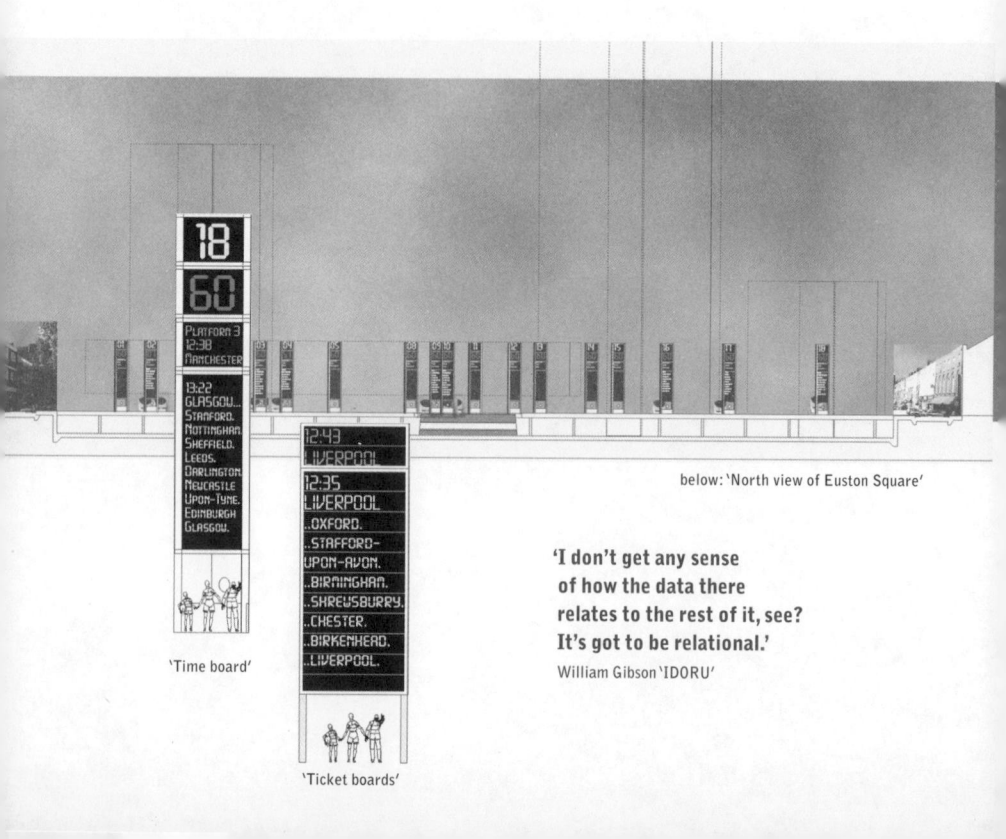

below: 'North view of Euston Square'

'Time board'

'Ticket boards'

> 'I don't get any sense of how the data there relates to the rest of it, see? It's got to be relational.'
> William Gibson 'IDORU'

'Main view with time board and fountain rooflights'

Peter Morris
MA in Architecture and Interiors: RCA
BA in AR: University of Plymouth

MAIN ENTRANCE TO TUBE SYSTEM UNDERGROUND MARKET THE UNDERPASS

'East view of Euston Station'

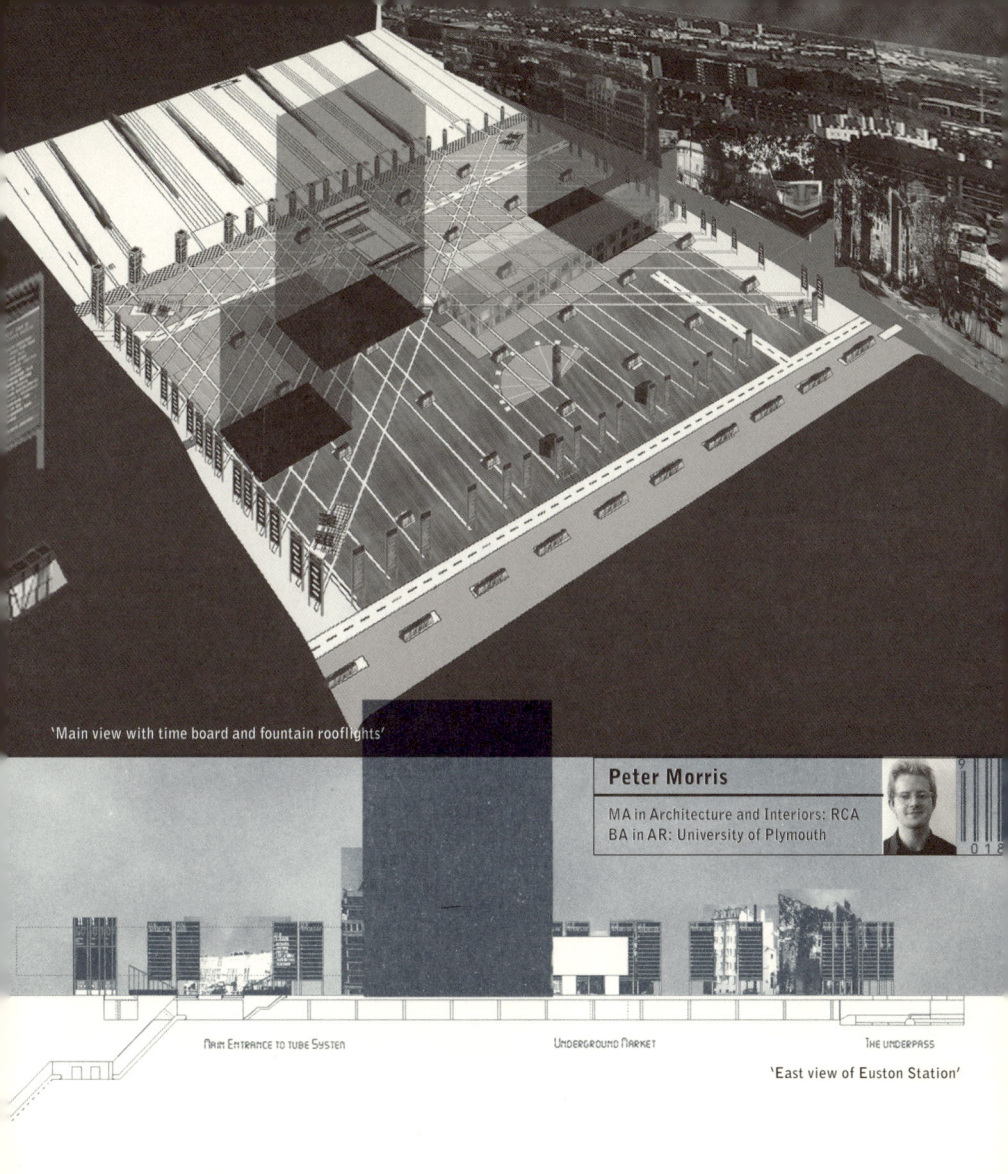

'UNFINISHED ARCHITECTURE'
Euston's Open Air Station and Public Square

Southwark has been a place of trade throughout the centuries, with the Borough Market functioning as a bridgehead to the City. The old London Bridge might serve as the most striking historical example for the social/economic setting of Southwark, with its hybrid architecture composed of public and private domains of offices, shops and housing.

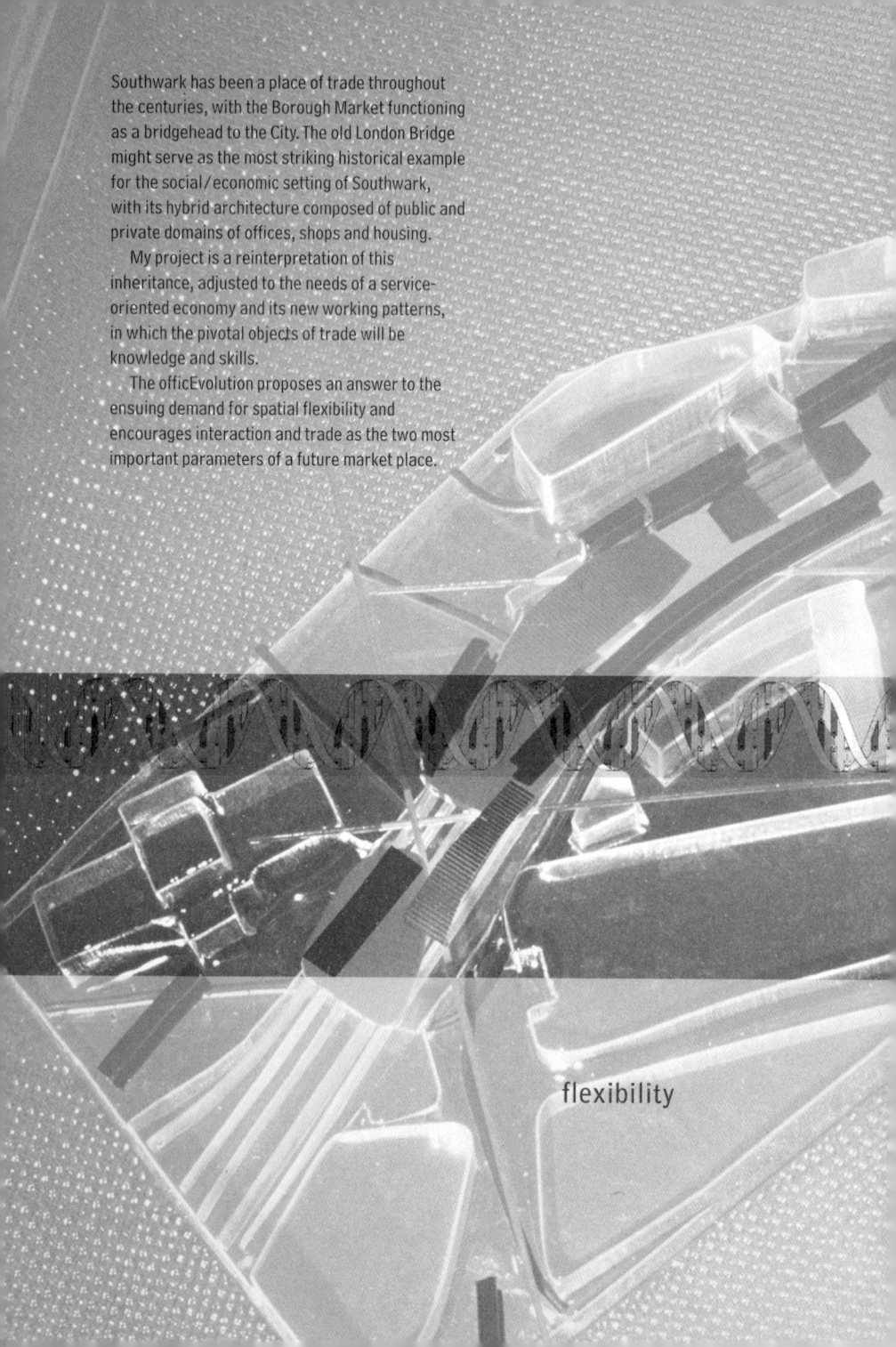

My project is a reinterpretation of this inheritance, adjusted to the needs of a service-oriented economy and its new working patterns, in which the pivotal objects of trade will be knowledge and skills.

The officEvolution proposes an answer to the ensuing demand for spatial flexibility and encourages interaction and trade as the two most important parameters of a future market place.

flexibility

interaction

OFFIC:E-SCAPE

Julia Thomas
MA in Architecture and Interiors: RCA
BA in AR: University of Applied Arts, Vienna

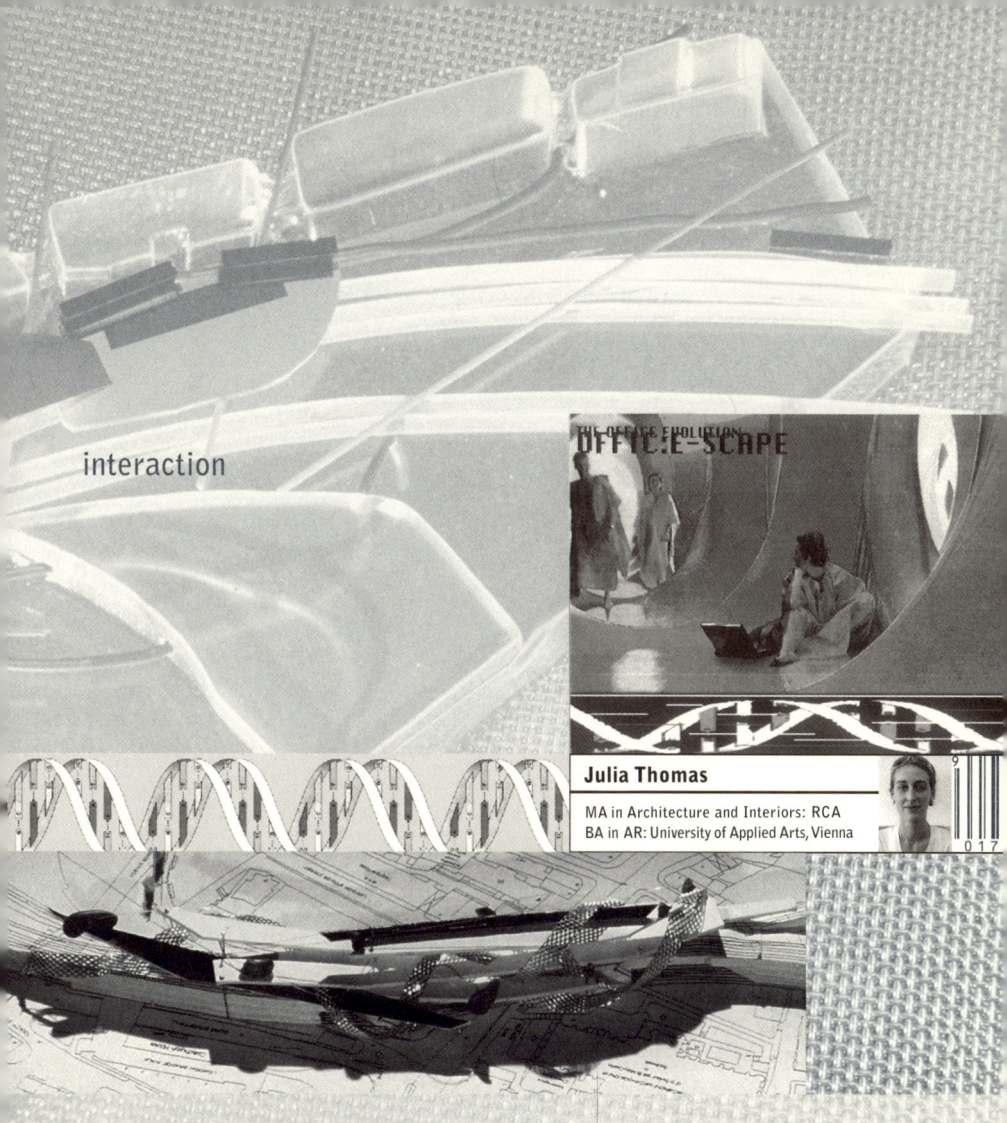

OfficEvolution
Future marketplace for Southwark

Euston station stands as an active transit zone in the broader Euston area in London. It functions as both a crossover point to the local surroundings as well as a strategic node or intensive focus for travellers. In addition to Euston's significant nodal character it also stands as a symbol of (trans)urban territorial escape, elaborating on its traditional role as the gateway to the North.

As a counteraction to the non-stop flux of the station, and referring to the aforementioned elements of Euston's identity, I propose a superimposition of relaxation layers to the existing strata of the station's activities in the form of territories. A series of floating, immersing and sound interfaces will offer a set of alternative body and mind activities to the traveller within a physical spacescape woven in the existing station structure. Encompassing fragments of actual and virtual territories, the relaxation layer will suggest a redefinition of the station's role and its relationship with the public piazza.

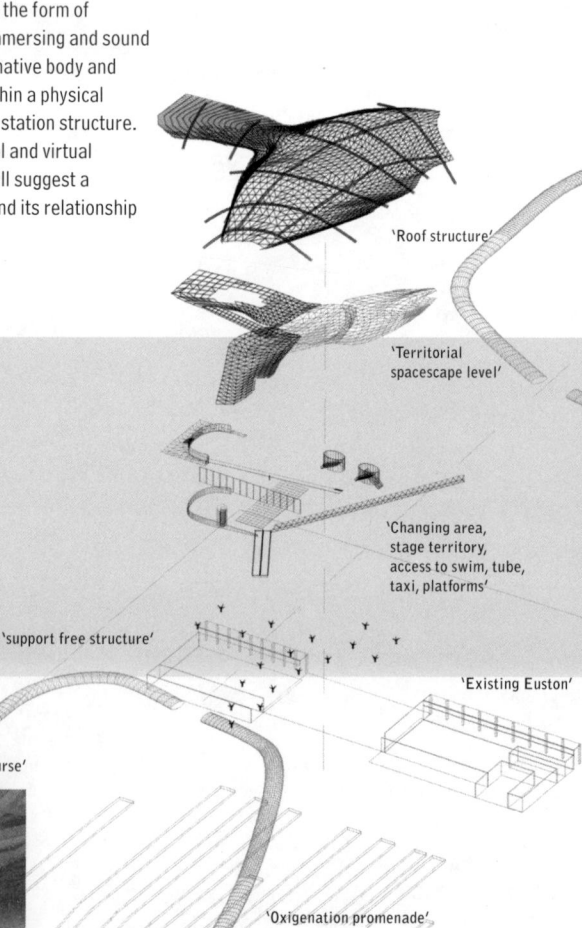

'Roof structure'

'Territorial spacescape level'

'Changing area, stage territory, access to swim, tube, taxi, platforms'

'support free structure'

'Existing Euston'

'Euston swimming ferritory concourse'

'Oxigenation promenade'

'Euston soundscape'

Redefining the station:
EUSTON RESUSCITATION TERRITORIES

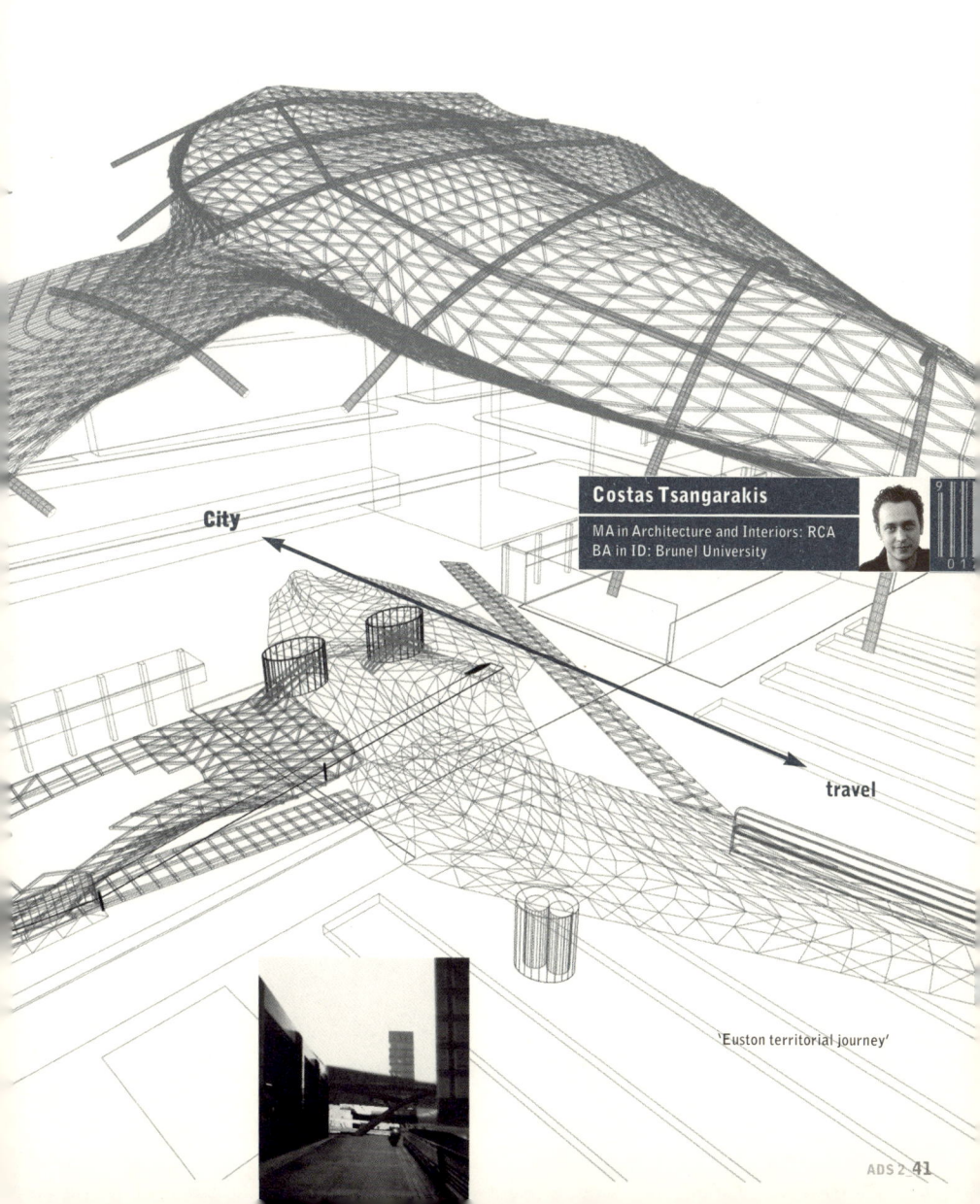

Costas Tsangarakis
MA in Architecture and Interiors: RCA
BA in ID: Brunel University

City

travel

'Euston territorial journey'

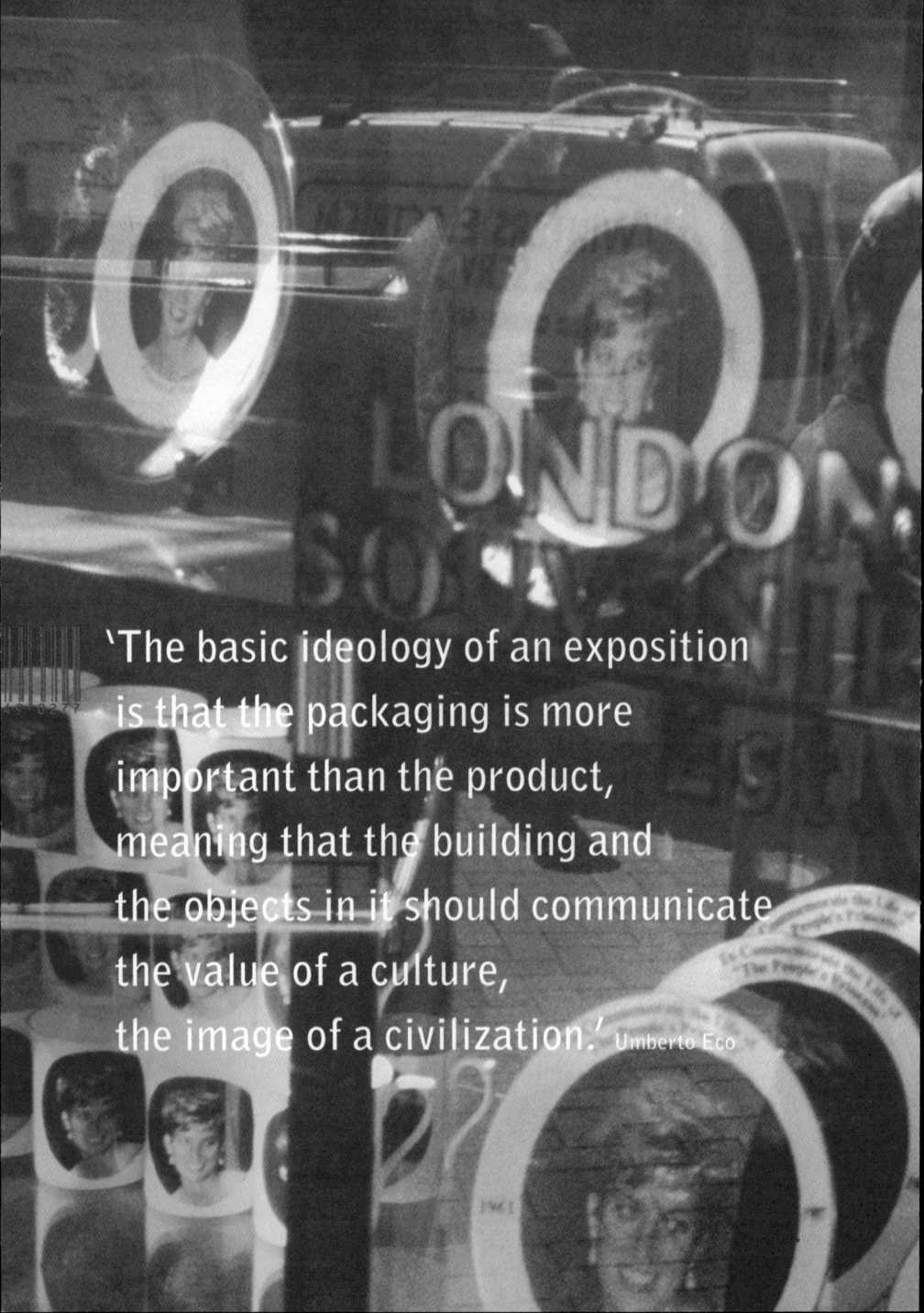

'The basic ideology of an exposition is that the packaging is more important than the product, meaning that the building and the objects in it should communicate the value of a culture, the image of a civilization.' Umberto Eco

ADSTHREE

expo(se):
Autobiography of a Nation

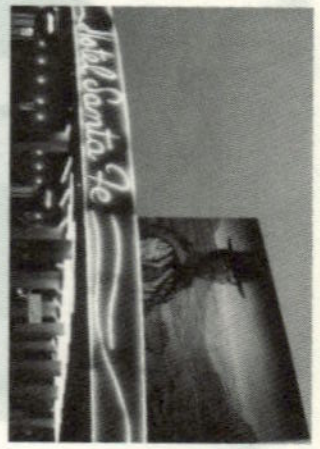

'Paris? Mexico? Where are you?'

Acknowledging that architecture is inscribed by its own image as much by the physicality of its own space, we spent the first term focussing our research on World Fairs and Expos which offer a fascinating insight into buildings as powerful symbolic messages.

The Great Millennium Yawn? Intrigued by the concept of World Fair but unenamoured by the latest institutionalised-fun-in-and-out-of-town-plastic-shed approach? Half a century on from the Festival of Britain, we have been exploring the core conditions at the heart of contemporary British culture using London as our base.

Term One includes a series of trips, talks and workshops devised to equip each student with the necessary tools and techniques to define the Unofficial Autobiography of a Nation. This later enables them to go on to produce designs for Expavilion - a building proposal where Form contaminates Function for Urban Event.

Their first task is to design and make an unofficial 'This is Britain' booklet for the millennium, the kind of thing you might find lurking at the back of Granny's drawer in fifty years time. We then take the Eurostar to Paris to meet the Secretary General of the BIE (Bureau International des Expositions) the official world Expo regulatory body, who gives us an intriguing talk covering the parameters of their powers to monitor and advise on all aspects of world fairs from overall themes to

Adam Scott: 'The Face of the Nation'

Johnny Wong: 'What do you remember?'

'Phrenology Head, colour chart'

'You are here'

'Wet weekend in Widness, wish you were here'

specific aspects of national pavilions. Even cocktails at the fabulously Baroque-encrusted bar at Le Train Bleu in the Gare du Lyon cannot prepare us for the unique experience of the Santa Fe Hotel - budget Mexicanarama Euro Disney style. Exhausted by our wild night of dry ice 'n' boogie at the Hurricane - Eurodisney's disco-from-hell - we spend the following morning with our official 'backstage' passes quizzing the in-house designers of Val d'Europe, the proposed new Disney town on the edge of the leisure park, a vast and extraordinary development which when completed will be a fifth the size of Paris. The afternoon is spent exploring the rides, collecting souvenirs and documenting the systems at work in the park dashing from one pavilion to another to avoid the Eurodrizzle.

Back on home soil we examine the booty of souvenirs from the Paris trip. As a group we look at the reductive iconographic messages at work in each object, analysing each souvenir as a memento of place or event and the point where function and memory collide. A workshop with fashion designers Antoni & Alison helps each student to then develop a prototype Souvenir for the year 2000 including graphics and packaging. Jonny's souvenirs are cast in blocks of ice like a frozen time capsule while Richard takes his cue from the Sensation exhibition at the Royal Academy and develops a souvenir range of Damien Hirst style food for Tescos.

Mark Gower: 'Pop-up pavillion'

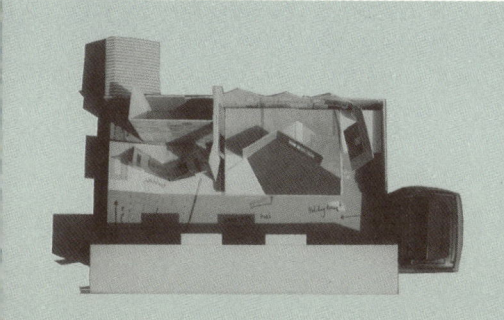

SALLY MACKERETH
AADipl, tutor of ADS 3
Wells Mackereth

DEBORAH SAUNT
BA DipArch, tutor of ADS 3
Deborah Saunt

CLIVE SALL
BA (Hons) DipArch, BA (Hons) Fine Art
Fashion Architecture Taste (FAT)

ADS 3 45

'Move over eurobland,
make way for the new albionism'

At this stage, we talk to Ben Evans from The Millennium Experience about the proposals for the Dome and the Demos Report which sets out the Government approved 'toolkit' for rebranding Britain. The students are then asked to formulate their own 'toolkit' as a brief to produce a design proposal for their Expavilion with three core components - a classic British institution, a characteristic of Britishness and a suitable urban site.

Spring term kicks off with a communication workshop with one of the designers from The Dome Experience where each student is coached to present their ideas in clear, direct language to a mythic millennium committee. As a group we spend a day building a giant urban scale model incorporating each of the proposals in relation to the Dome.

The rest of the term is spent generating ideas, proposing Unknown structures from Uncanny materials in Unlikely settings.

Inspired by Ghery's Guggenheim on their trip to Bilbao in March, the group return to London to hear that the BIE in Paris are keen to host an exhibition of ADS3 students' pavilions at the Lisbon Expo. Spurred on by the prospect of 'going public' with their work, the Expavilions rapidly take shape. The diversity of their form and content reveals a Portrait of a Nation rather different from Blair's Britannia: schemes include Dominic's finishing school for perplexed Lottery winners (page 55); Dome parasites abound in

Matt McNulty: 'Complainer', 'Booth Class', 'Closeup Booth', 'Bird Onblower'

'Take me higher'

the form of Mark's 'pack-up-n-leg-it' bootlegger's pavilion; Matt celebrates the great British trait of being deeply uncomfortable with the act of lodging a complaint; Ambridge farming methods have been applied to the South Bank in John's proposals (page53).

Finally, ADS3 celebrate the end of the year with a traditional British picnic with our union jack blanket straddling the longitude line in Greenwich park and the skeletal presence of the Dome looming appropriately in the background.

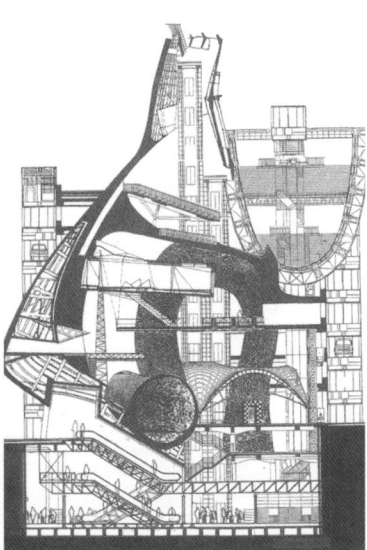

Tatiana Bacheva: 'Exclusiphere'

Tatiana Basheva
Richard Bassett
Dan Brill
Mark Gower
Richard Macrae
Alasdair McKenzie
Dominic McKenzie
Matthew McNulty
Bruce Peter
Adam Scott
Silvia Tonini
Johnny Wong

Sited behind the Millennium Dome, the Incidental Pavilion provides an alternative to the manufactured mass experience: appealing instead to the nation's natural curiosity.

The site has a steady flow of incidental visitors. The bridge is part of the Thames path, and the A102 is the main approach road into London from the South East.

The proposal provides these incidental visitors with a series of hypereal environments where everyday mundane events become frameworks for sensational happenings.

Banal objects and buildings across the site are enhanced, and their functions are altered to provide an environment where event is encouraged rather than dictated.

The Pub becomes a maximum security Police Station. The Road becomes an accident black spot. The Gas Works becomes a terrorist target.
The ordinary everyday is sensationalised, scrutinised, surveyed, and ultimately celebrated.

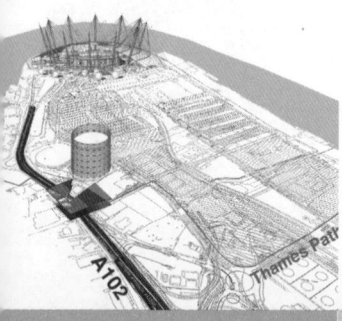

'Constant surveillance of the incidental', conceptual model

'From rural to riot and terrorism'

Richard Bassett
MA in Architecture and Interiors: RCA
BA in ID: Kingston University

INCIDENT(AL) PAVILION

ADS 3_49

In this alternative millennium proposal, the Royal Festival Hall (RFH) is seen as undergoing a permanent, slow-motion process of transformation. I have applied 'speculative' farming methods to the site in order to encourage wider public interest that will ultimately lead to a greater cultural understanding and freedom of expression.

If we think in terms of the RFH as a super postmodern farmhouse on steroids, then the City of London becomes the surrounding pastureland with flocks of human infested architecture grazing quietly nearby. The immediate metaphor has boundless connotations. The farmhouse, from previous research, remains a static, almost impassive element amongst the farm. Yet its role is pivotal - a kind of control centre of events. However, in the RFH's terms, the events are enclavic to the structure... the structure being enclavic to the South bank.

This interiority complex is ideal for a rural programme to be implanted.

Have you ever had sex in a field?

'Muck spreading', 'Clip and dip', 'Crop rotation', 'Grouping (herd)', 'Homely'

John Blanchard
MA in Architecture and Interiors: RCA
BA in ID: Kingston University

2:00   3:00   4:00   5:00   6:00   7:00   8:00   9:00   10:00   11:00   12:00

The year 2000 is in itself simply a unit of measure, therefore it carries no inherent significance of its own. So how can it be made into an eventful and meaningful experience?

Time has no known beginning or end, thus to celebrate the millennium is to celebrate the manmade constructs which organise time, rather than time itself. These constructs, or measures, form the paradox by which the proposal has taken shape. Time zones, solar energy, clocks, and satellite communications technology are combined in the proposal to expose their opposites: the unmeasurable, infinite.

The proposal consists of 24 pavilions, one in each time zone around the globe. Each pavilion is a live audio and visual link to every other pavilion. The individual spectator may interact directly, at full scale, with another spectator at any of the other 23 pavilions; have a chat, pull a face, practice your Cantonese or Arabic. Creating a direct line from the individual to the global, the proposal becomes a kind of 'real time' machine, not of the past or future, but of the present.

Representing the totality of one complete revolution of the earth on its axis, the pavilions each reveal all hours of day and night, simultaneously. Thus, the effect of perpetual dawn is generated, passing gently from frame to frame.

'The earth is our clock...
One, thirty, three hundred and sixty five, those are the units by which our undertakings must be measured.'
Le Corbusier

THROUGH THE LOOKING GLASS
(It's always midnight somewhere in the world)
Proposal for the Millennium

Daniel Brill
MA in Architecture: Royal College of Art
BA in AR: Southbank University

If, as has often been said, dogs resemble their owners and bearing in mind the fact that Britain is a nation of dog lovers, my proposal suggests that a dogs home can be understood as a metaphor for Britain.

From society's underdogs housed in Battersea Dogs Home-style cages at the bottom, to the Top Dogs living in the lap of luxury upstairs, Bond Street Dogs Home expresses notions of pedigree and class intimately associated with both the world of dogs and Bond Street.

Across a bridge from the Dogs Home stands the National Lottery Winner's Finishing School. Here, Lottery Winners are taught how to cope with their new found wealth. Lessons range from financial investment, to which knife and fork to use at a formal dinner, to how one addresses a Baron. There's a lot to learn if they are to avoid appearing (horror!) nouveau riche.

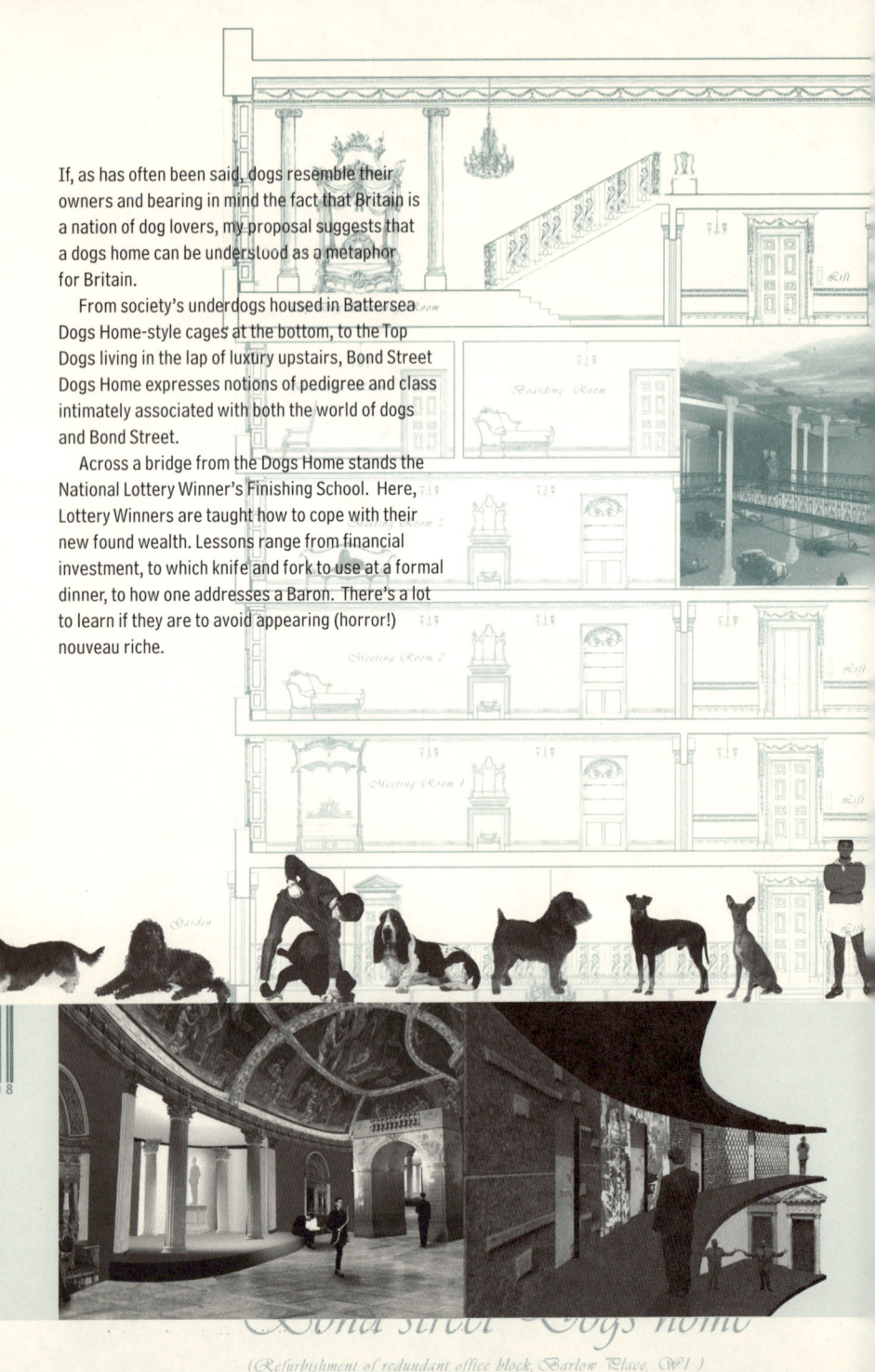

Bond Street Dogs Home
(Refurbishment of redundant office block, Barlow Place, W1)

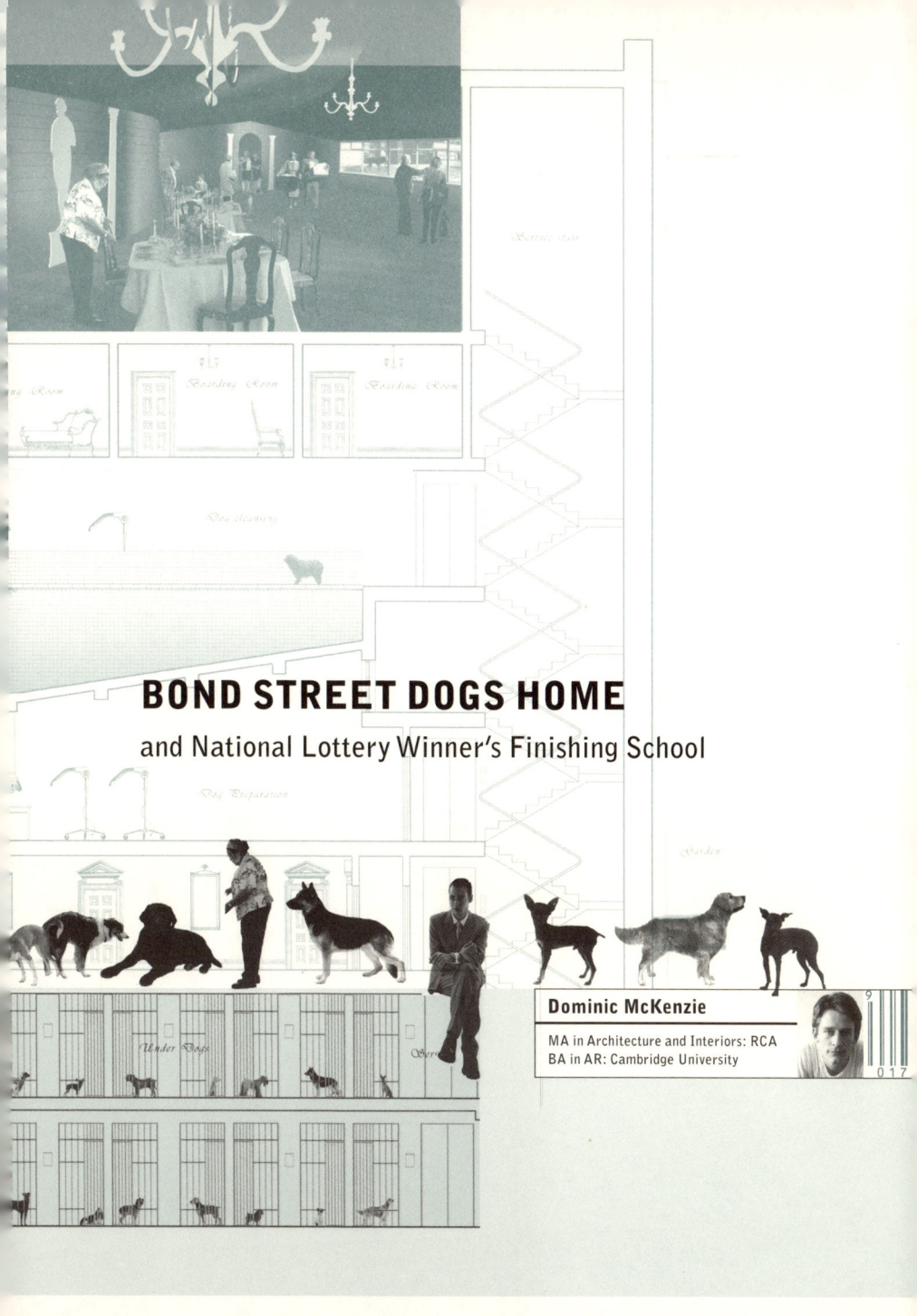

BOND STREET DOGS HOME
and National Lottery Winner's Finishing School

Dominic McKenzie

MA in Architecture and Interiors: RCA
BA in AR: Cambridge University

An URBAN EVENT celebrating the British love of HORSE RACING and GARDENING transforming two miles of abandoned railway viaducting from Liverpool Street to Dalston into a landscaped race course and park...

Betting and Gardening involve chance, luck and skill. The spectacle of flat racing through high rise housing estates, over railway bridges, past mosques and through industrial wasteland will be interwoven with the splendour of five different interpretations of the English Garden. These act as threshholds, conditioning the atmosphere of the event. The rhetorics of famous garden designers - from Capability Brown to Dan Pearson - are re-interpreted for a modern urban environment. A series of pavilions, using re-scaled and re-programmed garden buildings, allow a wide diversity of people to enjoy the event - Burger King and bouncy castles to royal receptions and champagne luncheons. Using the camera as a link, social and cultural boundaries may be momentarily suspended and people's perceptions of their surroundings changed through the shared experience of the race.

'2.20 at Haggerston'

'Jockey Club Megashed'

'4.30 at Haggerston'

ASCOT IN THE CITY

Bruce Peter
MA in Architecture and Interiors: RCA
BA in ID: Glasgow School of Art

'De Beauvoir Hills Stadium'

The proposal:
A bridge where language is exhibited, celebrated and performed. Language as instrument of sensuous communication, language as intellectual playground, language as bridge between the real and the unreal.

The site:
London, where the Thames and the Meridian line cross (next to the Millennium Dome). The river as an inspiration for alternating movement (tide) and unstable forces (stream).

The structure:
Using the Braille language as programmatic and structural device. The structure of the Braille alphabet consists of dots and lines which are interpreted as moments and fields.

The activity:
Travelling as psycological experience, moving as if being inside Babbage's archetypal computer to connect the visitors to an unusual aspect of language.

'Programmatic plan and model of bridge'

Fragment 'Pathos'

'Meridian communication line'

LAN[D]GUAGE
Unofficial Millennium Pavilion

Silvia Tonini
MA in Architecture and Interiors: RCA
BA in AR: Florence University

Floating Island 'Forest with talking trees'

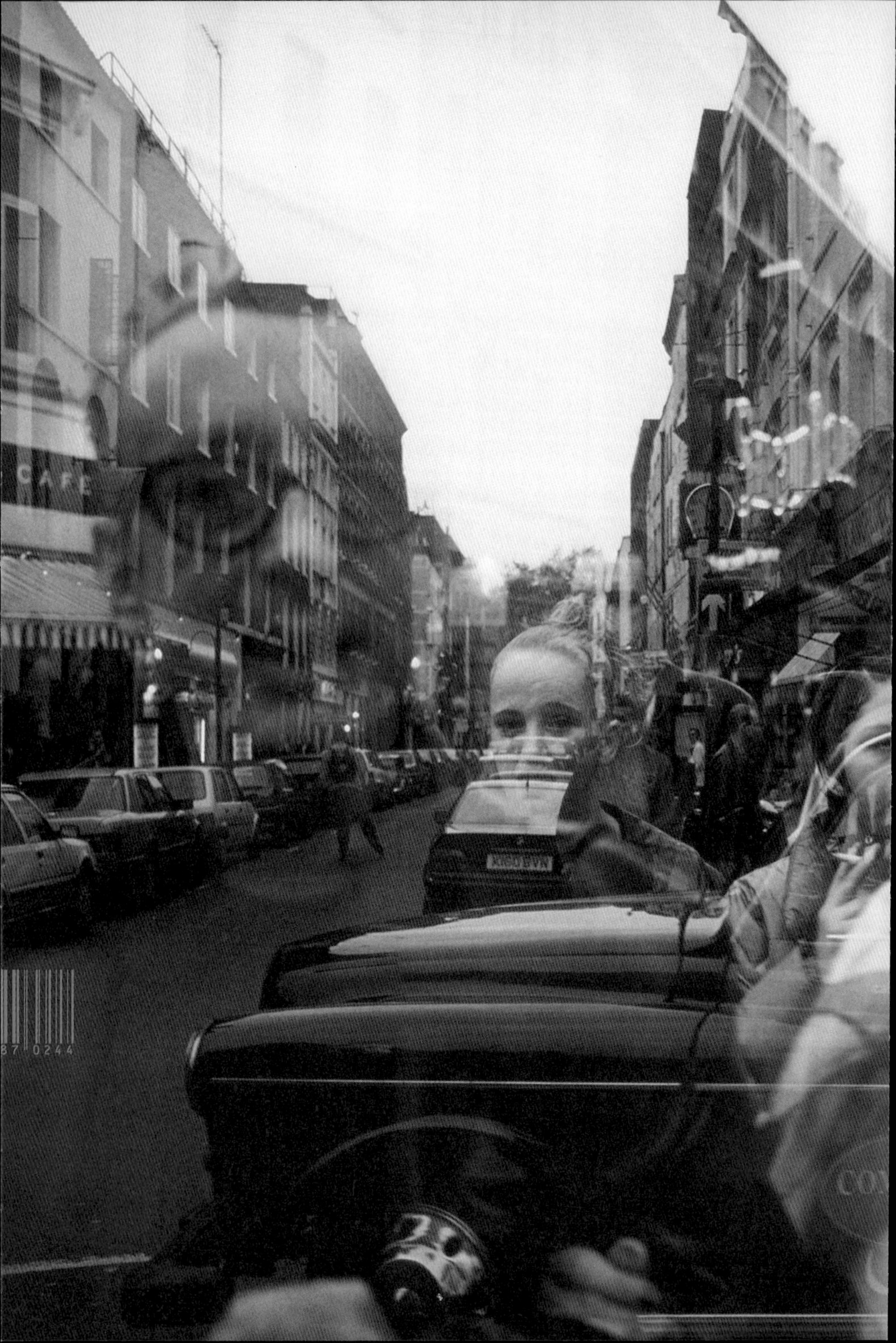
CAFE
87 0244

'Interactivity between occupant and architecture, both as correlating parts of a dynamic system that seems to be alive – that is viable architecture.'

Peter Weibel
in 'Christian Möller - Interaktive Architektur'

Since early experiments with bubble-based inflatable forms in the sixties, very little has changed in the field of pneumatics. Practical application of air supported structures has been limited for reasons of structural unreliability, complexity of manufacture and lack of spatial diversity. Recent advances in biotechnology, mathematical modelling of complex systems, computer-aided design and an upsurge of interest in high-tech materials led me to look at pneumatics from a new angle. Using high-tech pattern cutting techniques from the fashion industry I developed a series of asymmetrical structural inflatable shapes based on a cross-fertilisation of advanced technologies from these fields. By tackling the feasibility of architectural use of pneumatics, at a time of new interest in temporary and portable structures, I hope to shed new light on the potential of an entirely different and exciting architectural form.

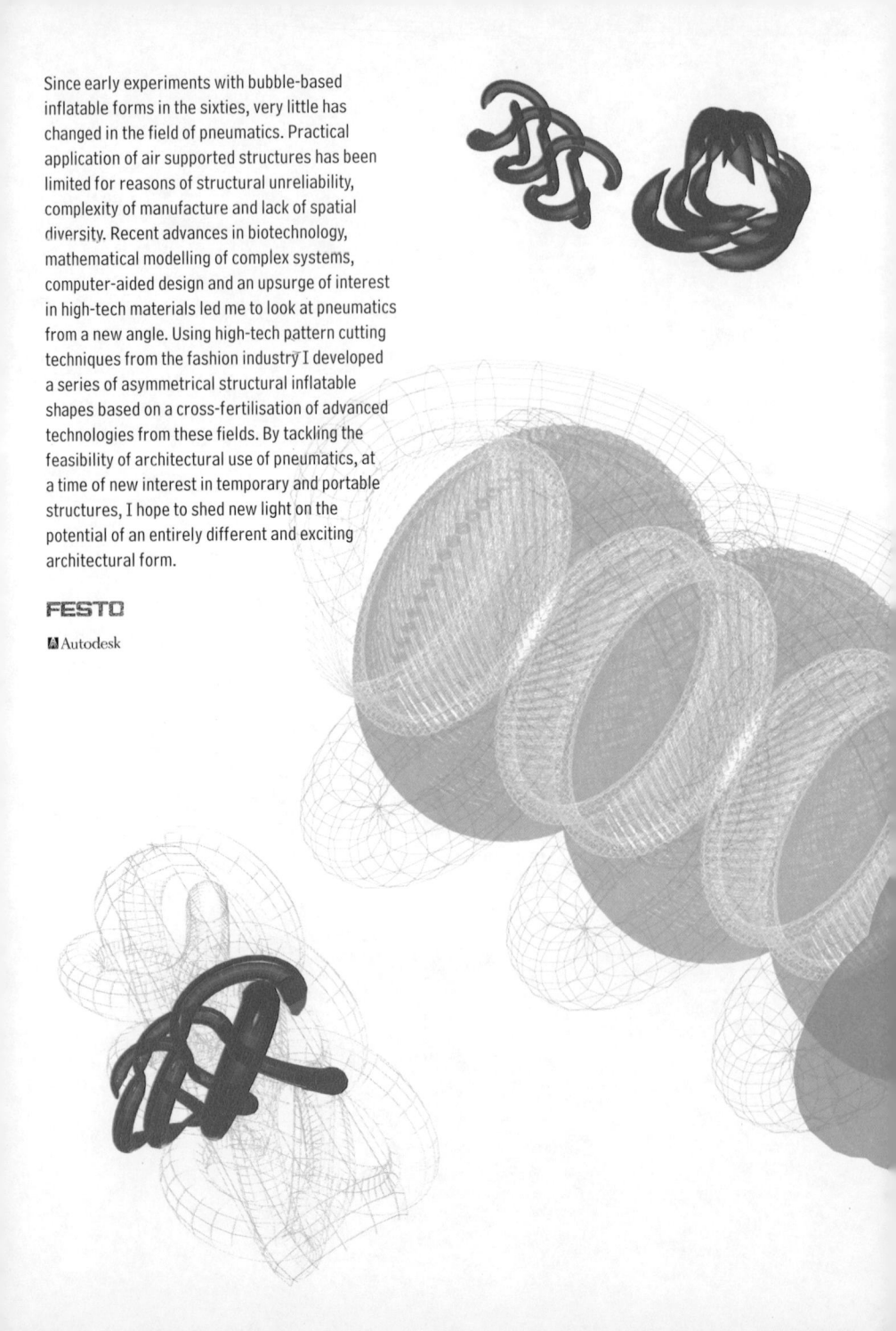

FESTO

Autodesk

Judit Kimpian, Research

MPhil. Research at the RCA, MA (RCA)
BA (Hons): University of Westminster

PNEUMATIX

Architecture and Interiors

Course Director
Professor Nigel Coates

Development
Claire Catterall

Cultural Events
Ben Evans

ADS1
Knut Hovland, Fiona Raby

ADS2
John Smith, Andrew Onraët, Olivier Védrine

ADS3
Sally Mackereth, Deborah Saunt, Clive Sall

Comprehensive Design Project
Matthew Lloyd, Julian Cripps
Charles McBeath (External Examiner)

Professional Practice
Jamie Campbell

Humanities Tutor
Brian Hatton

MA External Examiners
Will Alsop, Eva Jiricna

Visiting Professor
Daniel Libeskind

Computing Technician
Patrick Russell

Course Secretary
Máiréad McDermott

Darwin Workshop technical support
Kevin Adams, Boyd Costen, Malcolm Chave,
Jeff Footman, Peter Longfellow, Robert Loupart,
Martin Raxworthy

Consultant Engineers
Michael Coombes, Alax Baxter & Associates
Carolina Bartram, Atelier 1
Jeff Parkes and Mike Cook, Buro Happold
Tim Macfarlene and Stephen Bandy, Dewhurst Macfarlane
Brian Mark, Fulcrum Engineering
Max Fordham and David Lindsay, Max Fordham & Ptns
Michael Edwards and Tim McCaul, Ove Arup & Ptns
Tom Lloyd and Luke Pearson, Pearson Lloyd
Nick Hannika and Robert Myers, Price & Myers
Simon Bourne, Robert Benaim & Associates
Mike Hadi, Techniker Engineering
Mike Poulard, Charles McBeath and Mark Whitby,
Whitby & Bird

Guest Lecturers

David Batchelor
Mark Brearley
Tyler Brûlé
Robin Clark
Paul Finch
Prof. Christopher Frayling
Mark Garside
Ron Geesin
Piers Gough
SeanGriffiths
Charlie Hussey
Paul Karakusevic
Light Surgeons Ltd
Jeremy Lord
John Lyall
Robert Mull
Ted Polhemus
Craig Riley
Peter Silver
Oliver Solway
Graham Watson
Tom Whitehead
Philip Wilson
Carlos Villanueva-Brandt
Roger Zogolovitch

Guest Critics

Sebastian Bergne
Doug Branson
Ellen Cantor
Paul Davies
Alex de Rijke
Lisa Fior
Jason Griffiths
Philip Gumuchdjian
Gillian Horne
Ben Kelly
Catherine Martin
Alicia Pavaro
James Soane
Toni Spencer
Neil Spiller
Theodore Zeldin

Cybaroque Series

John Thackara
Ron Arad
Pier Luigi Capucci
Lars Spuybroek
Laurie Anderson
Christian Möller
Elisabeth Diller
Zaha Hadid

Awards and sponsors

Alsop & Störmer
Brintons Carpets
Boyden & Co
Dazed and Confused
Dulux ICI
Din Associates
Sue & Terry Farrell
Festo AG & Co
J & B Bombay Sapphire
Rutters for Scanachrome
Trebruk Marketing Limited,
Munkedals AB, Sweden